Text and Context

Praise for *Text and Context: The Operative Word*

"A good read, direct and simple, loaded with useful material."
— *Guillermo Verdecchia — playwright, director and educator*

"A wonderful guide for theatre makers, and not just directors and actors. It's totally applicable to design students as well, and I plan on using this book when I teach."
— *Kelly Wolf, theatre designer and educator*

"Richard's book is a testament to the care, joy and precision evident in his works on stage. In each clear step he lays it out for you like a trusted mentor; familiar and funny and thick with honesty and opinion."
— *Jillian Keiley, Artistic Director—English Theatre, Canada's National Arts Centre*

"There is a lot of useful material out there on directing, but if you can only read one book before embarking on your next project, make it this one. It's practical, entertaining, and rigorous without being judgmental. Kind of the definition of good directing."
— *Miles Potter, director*

"Even though he has been practicing his art for forty-five years, Richard is in the vanguard of the new, compassionate and collaborative philosophy of directing. Young directors, and those who just need reminders of good practice and some well-structured advice, will benefit hugely from this book. As I read through the book, some of Richard's guidance awoke me to my own mistakes in practice and I am grateful for that. An old dog can learn new tricks!"
— *Judith Thompson, playwright, director, educator*

"My personal copy of this book will have my emphatic underlinings and the word 'Yes!!!' scribbled all over the margins. Greenblatt offers erudition, practical insights and compassionate advice to his fellow theatre makers, as well as entertaining and illuminating anecdotes from his four decades as an actor, director and teacher, without a hint of bullshit."
— *Seana McKenna, actor, director, and educator*

"Being a director can be a lonely enterprise despite how deeply collaborative it is. Unlike actors, we rarely get to spend time in each other's rooms and processes. I'm grateful to Richard Greenblatt for pulling back the curtains on his process — a process that has established itself and evolved through wearing many hats and living many lives. *Text and Context: The Operative Word* offers practitioners a direct and compassionate map to follow with a simultaneous invitation to find one's own road."
— *Andrea Donaldson, Artistic Director, Nightwood Theatre*

"Richard gifts us with a pragmatic directorial process that exemplifies collaboration rather than hierarchy. He says it best himself: 'Most of the best directing I do is providing context for others to do their best work.' I look forward to watching the work of the next generation of directors who are guided by his principles."
— *Jani Lauzon, director, playwright, and educator*

"With *Text and Context*, Richard Greenblatt offers concrete and immediately applicable approaches to creating a process that is sensitive, dynamic and transparent. A gift to theatre practitioners."
—*Alisa Palmer, Artistic Director, English Section, National Theatre School of Canada*

Text and Context

The Operative Word

*A Handbook for Script Work
and Directing in the Theatre*

Richard Greenblatt

J. GORDON SHILLINGFORD
PUBLISHING INC

Text and Context : The Operative Word
first published 2021 by J. Gordon Shillingford Publishing Inc.
© 2021 Richard Greenblatt

Scirocco Drama Editor: Glenda MacFarlane
Cover design by Doowah Design
Photo of Richard Greenblatt by Cylla von Tiedemann

Printed and bound in Canada on 100% post-consumer recycled paper.
We acknowledge the financial support of the Manitoba Arts Council and
The Canada Council for the Arts for our publishing program.

Library and Archives Canada Cataloguing in Publication

Title: Text & context : the operative word : a handbook for script work and direct-
ing in the theatre / Richard Greenblatt.
Other titles: Text and context I Handbook for script work and directing in the
theatre
Names: Greenblatt, Richard, 1952- author.
Identifiers: Canadiana 20210136391 I ISBN 9781927922736 (softcover)
Subjects: LCSH: Theater—Production and direction—Handbooks, manuals, etc.
Classification: LCC PN2053 .G74 2021 I DDC 792.02/33—dc23

J. Gordon Shillingford Publishing
P.O. Box 86, RPO Corydon Avenue, Winnipeg, MB Canada R3M 3S3

To all Canadian theatre practitioners,
who toil without much hope of great
financial reward or fame. They make me
proud to be a member of our community.

CONTENTS

Foreword 11

Preface 15

PART ONE ——TEXT

1 What Is a Word? 21
2 Getting Started 26
3 The Operative Word 38
4 The Exercises 51

PART TWO ——CONTEXT

5 What Is Directing? 67
6 Pre-Production 73
7 Rehearsal 86
8 Scheduling 110
9 Talking to Actors... 116
10 ...And Others 132
11 After Opening 141
12 Director Training 148

Part Three ——New Text

13 Theatre for Young Audiences 157
14 New Plays 166
15 Devised Work 181

Afterword 201

Acknowledgments 203

Foreword

I am a playwright, a director, an actor, a deviser and a Professor of Theatre; the fashionable term for all those practices is "theatre maker," but something about that term makes me cringe. So, I do all those things, but I'm going to talk to you about Richard's brilliant book on directing from my perspective as a *playwright*.

A famously *difficult* playwright.

I have had a terrible time with directors, from the very beginning of my adventures in the Canadian theatre scene. I often feel they are messing up and misunderstanding my play. They often feel that I am interfering and disrespectful of theatrical protocol. Guilty! If a director is pushing the actor to misrepresent the substance of the play and twist the text, it is my job to be the protector of the text. I have been banned from rehearsal rooms, yelled at, and quietly despised for my interfering ways. There are only a few directors that I know did a better job than I would have in directing my work, and Richard Greenblatt is one of them.

Richard is one of the few directors who knocked me out with his vision of my work. Watching his productions, I did not feel the urge to take a single note, to correct anything, or to wince; rather, I sat there in awe, sometimes thinking *"Oh, this is what I meant when I wrote that! Thank you, Richard!"* His work on both *Lion in the Streets* and *Elektra* was dazzling. He works with a deep understanding of text, of psychological motivation, of the organic poetry of human speech, and of theatricality. *Richard knows what he is doing.*

When I wrote my first play, *The Crackwalker*, on a typewriter and handed it, full of white-out and scribbles in the margins, to a wise mentor, Michael Mawson (who Richard quotes), I was beyond thrilled when he showed a passionate interest in it. We met at coffee shops and he gave me some excellent dramaturgical advice, and then he shopped the play around every theatre in the city. They all turned it down, saying it was too raw, too vulgar and way too depressing. Nobody wanted to see these "sad, vulgar" people on stage! Finally, Keith Turnbull, the artistic director of NDWT, expressed interest. He granted us a workshop, and other than the birth of my children, it was the most exciting moment of my life. These superb professional actors actually inhabited a world that I had created. The production that followed at Theatre Passe Muraille was a resounding, life-changing success, despite, or maybe because of, the draining daily conflict between the director and me. I will always be grateful to that director for taking on the play when no one else would.

Richard would never, ever declare war on a playwright. As he writes in the book, he has immense respect for the playwright and the work that they have produced. He desires only to serve and protect and enhance and explore the play he is directing. For example: many directors will actually black out the stage directions, but Richard looks very carefully at them, because he understands that they are an integral part of the playwright's vision. He understands if the direction is "both George and Laura freeze," that that means two separate and unique moments. Richard will guide each actor carefully: what are they thinking as individuals, how does Laura freeze differently than George, and why? Another example from the book: I was very struck by his thinking about the word "conversation," in what seems like almost a throwaway line in an early scene from *Lion in the Street*: Bill says to his desperate wife: "I'll just finish this conversation, and then I'll come." Richard points out that the root of the word "conversation" means "to live with" but it was also a word used to refer to intercourse. Richard believes that when a playwright is working from their finest dramatic instinct, they will choose words that are more right for the moment than even they consciously know.

What a gift to a playwright.

Most helpfully, *Text and Context: The Operative Word* is a superb directing manual. When teaching directing in the past, I have found myself floundering—should I show them what I do, or several methods, or let them just dive in? Richard's book is a perfect solution. It does instruct us on how to direct, but it leaves ample room for one's own unique approach and interpretation of a text. A student who follows Richard's step-by-step instruction will serve the play and the actors and the designers very well indeed. What a relief to have a book like this!

Richard provides us with delicious and helpful quotations, the kind of wisdom actors gleefully pass back and forth in the dressing room: he quotes the famous Alfred Lunt and Lynn Fontane story about asking for the tea instead of the laugh. It is so true — as soon as an actor seems to be asking for a laugh, they will not get one. The audience is quite feral in this way. Richard knows this and insists that his actor's objective is not to be praised, but to climb inside the character they are playing and do what the character is meant to be doing in the play.

I have never had a passion for directing. I only direct my own work to be certain that the premiere production is the play that I wrote. If Richard Greenblatt was around and willing to direct, I would definitely choose him! Directors such as Richard can create a production that brings more depth and beauty and nuance than even I knew my play had.

A director must be a leader, but never a tyrant. The old way I experienced as I was in training and at the beginning of my career was for directors to be fascist dictators, reducing actors to tears, and pitting them against each other. Richard believes in collaboration, in respecting not only the playwright but the actors and the designers too. He sums up his philosophy of directing in inspiring ways, and even though he has been practising his art for forty-five years, Richard is in the vanguard of the new, compassionate and collaborative philosophy of directing. Young directors, and those who just need reminders of good practice and some well-structured advice, will benefit hugely from this book. As I read through the book, some of Richard's guidance awoke me to my own mistakes in practice and I am grateful for that. An old dog can learn new tricks!

We theatre makers of 2021 are experiencing the most challenging year since the pandemic of 1918; every theatre in this country has been closed since last March. Some resourceful souls have pivoted and found new ways of making a good living, from cookie baking, to teaching, to mask making, to tech start-ups, but the flame of theatre is burning in our collective soul, and when theatre is back, we will be here, ready to take up the torch.

I am a sixty-six-year-old playwright now working on a novel; however, I have not abandoned the theatre. When the right story presses to be told through the theatre, I will tell it. And Richard Greenblatt, if I'm lucky, will direct it.

Judith Thompson

Preface

Why this book?

It was mostly written well before the COVID crisis, and I must admit that I have faith that we will return to some semblance of pre-virus "normal" social distancing eventually. If we do not, then so many rules will have changed that all of the behaviours we have taken for granted for so long will be so drastically altered as to be unrecognizable to our pre-crisis selves. If that is the case, then the very nature of live theatre will have to be completely redefined, and that's just not this book.

This book is firstly about how I've been developing and using the method of text investigation and its exercises as laid out in **Part 1 — Text**, for over forty-five years as a director and dramaturg, and that writers, designers and especially actors seem to find helpful in the beginning steps toward building their work. I have been encouraged to write it down by colleagues, friends and family before I either get too old to remember it, or I die. It is a method mostly of my own invention, but also includes some adaptations of exercises from others, and has been tested by trial and error over many years in productions that I've directed. It has developed slowly, and I have changed, honed and shaped it over time until I have found what works best for me and my ability to communicate it to my colleagues. I now use it consistently much as it appears in the following pages.

The later exercises in Chapter 4 (Exercises #4 and up) I use only when working with students or young professionals. Experienced actors usually have their own methodology of discovering the physical and/or the inner life of the characters they are playing.

If they don't, it is unlikely they would have survived as working actors. The communal text work, however, I always use. It is very occasionally met with initial skepticism, but usually after less than fifteen minutes or so, that attitude inevitably changes. It is amazing what a little empowerment and actually dealing with the text and its issues will produce in actors.

These methods and exercises are meant to be exceedingly pragmatic, and not theoretical or academic in any way. Text analysis, at least as I define it for theatre practitioners, is meant to be used as a way to help the artist decipher the words a playwright has written and make them come alive — literally — on stage. The actors give them breath and complexity, designers give them a world in which to inhabit, while the director gives them the glue — or context — to bind them all together into a somewhat coherent and consistent world. Scripts are puzzles, and the artists who interpret these hieroglyphs must first ask the right questions before they start making any decisions on how their inimitable interpretation will be realized.

Part 2 — Context is about various ideas, philosophies and precepts I have about directing for the stage. There are a lot of misconceptions about the nature of the position of director, and when young people start directing, they are often hindered by these assumptions and by some traditional definitions that are irrelevant, or worse, harmful to establishing a creative process. I'm assuming that these thoughts may be more useful to newer directors than to more experienced ones. But who knows?

I've structured this section based on the order and rhythm of most rehearsal processes, minus the text work as outlined in Part 1. For me, each and every aspect of this process — from initial discussions to final performance — is interrelated. The precepts of communication with all of one's collaborators are the same, even if the specific individuals and their needs are variable. In this way, the form and content of the art form are completely connected. Content works best when it is rigorously and uniquely specific. So too does the way that content is interpreted and presented. And so too is the communication that directors employ with all their collaborators.

Part 3 — New Text grew out of separate but equally relevant aspects of both text work and directing. Theatre for Young Audiences (Chapter 13) is, in my mind, a specialized genre that is often overlooked by many theatre practitioners, or worse, denigrated as something less than theatre for adults. Nothing can be further from the truth in my opinion, as I will iterate in the chapter.

Many of the principles of text analysis are extremely useful in the development of new plays (Chapter 14), but of course, the circumstances are different. It also deals with the added responsibility of being a dramaturg that most directors assume, including during the practice of workshopping. The ways of interpreting the words that the writer has provided are similar to a "finished" script, but the aims of this process might directly and immediately affect the creation itself.

Similarly, a lot of the directing I describe in Part 2 — Context is used in the creation of devised work (Chapter 15), but again, the circumstances are different. In this case, you are directing artists who are both the creators as well as the actors, and so the outcome is simultaneously the creation and the interpretation of the work.

The process of artistic creation is a bottomless pit. I have spent my entire career working on and thinking about how I work and how to make my work better, and I feel there is still much more to discover. Theatre is a never-ending struggle to create and recreate the world anew, and how you create is at least as important as what you create and will undoubtedly affect the quality of the creation.

So. Here it is. My book. I hope whoever you are, you will find it useful.

PART ONE

TEXT

1

—

What Is a Word?

Language is amazing. (Like, duh!) How different cultures have found different sounds to create a shared vocabulary among their group and develop references, metaphors and complex ideas to communicate so intimately and so relatively quickly is truly mind-boggling.

And yet, language has myriad pitfalls, and leads to a plethora of misunderstandings, even in — or perhaps especially in — the most intimate of relationships. Certain words or phrases are triggers to extreme emotional reactions. A single word can hurt, elevate, inspire, dehumanize, or start a war.

A word is a symbol: a representation of an object, idea, action, or emotion. It is quicker and easier to say "chair" than it is to say, "that thing that is often human-made that we sit on."

And words come with a ton of baggage.

O O O

Let's go back to the chair: close your eyes and imagine a chair.

What does it look like? What is it made of? Where is it? In a room or out of doors? If in a room, which room? What is the rest of the decor like? Do you like this room? How does it make you feel? If the chair is outside, where is it? What's the weather like? Does this chair belong to someone you know? Does it belong to you? Do you often sit in it? Or never? What do you do if and when you sit in it? Is it comfortable? Does this chair still exist, and if so, where is it? How do you physically feel when you sit in it? And how do you feel emotionally? Does it make you feel safe? Anxious? Powerful? Insecure?

o o o

All these memories, feelings, and primal urges emanate from the word, "chair." And this is one's first instinctive impression, without preconceived thought or conscious choice of a particular chair. It could have been any chair, but for some unknown reason, this is the chair that emerged in your mind's eye at this moment in time. Most importantly, it is as individual and specific as you yourself, the person who imagined it.

So, when a playwright writes that word, and when a director and a designer and an actor begin to interpret that word, where do they start? Can they possibly know what chair the playwright was envisioning? Are there clues elsewhere in the text? If not, do you go to a chair you know in your memory as a starting point, or do you start with a "blank," neutral chair — whatever that is — and begin a journey of discovery for the quintessential chair, at least in the context of this story?

Now, in a particular play, the word "chair" may or may not be significant. It may or may not have resonance (a word which I will use often in this book) to which attention must needs be paid. But what about the word "love"? That's almost always pretty significant. What about "family"? "Child"? "Work"? "Sex"? "Politics"? I could go on…

So, words contain worlds within them, and tangential tendrils of thoughts, emotions and imaginative flights of consciousness and subconsciousness all encompassed in their makeup.

They truly are symbols, greater than the sum of their parts, deeper than their literal or surface meaning, and more often than not, possess both intended and unintended resonance.

Etymology

I am a bit of an etymological nerd. I believe much is learned from understanding the origin of a word: its original meaning, its cultural history and its relation to other forms of the same root word. For example: the word "text" comes from the same root as "texture" and is sometimes used to indicate the scriptures (which contains the word "script"). It comes from the Latin *texere*, meaning "to weave." Strands woven together (textiles) to create one piece of fabric. "Script" comes from *scribere*, meaning "to write." Hence, written strands.

The words become a phrase, the phrase becomes a sentence, the sentence is put with others and placed in a "context" (literally, "with text"), until the material is woven, combined with other pieces, and cut and sewn together to ultimately create...something. A garment, perhaps. Or something else. But it starts with a single thread.

Specificity

What we are desperately seeking as theatrical interpreters is specificity. We want to escape the obvious, the cliché, the mundane, and often — but not always — the first choice. That way lies generic and uninteresting art. The difference in content between Chekov and a TV soap opera is not very significant on the surface. But underneath, the difference is huge. Chekov wrote about his characters in their place and time and circumstances: inimitably middle-class Russia in the late 19th and early 20th centuries. And because they are so specifically and well written, his plays speak to everyone around the world in the 21st century, because we can put ourselves in these characters' situations and empathize with their dilemmas. That is the power of great theatrical writing. Any writing. Any art.

Soap opera doesn't last much longer than its rather short shelf life because its characters are generic, and their dilemmas are dealt with in obvious and predictable ways, or sometimes in outrageous and unbelievable ways. The drama is not gut-wrenching because it is way too easy, and nothing is truly "earned." Now, to be fair, I don't think that the writers, directors, actors and producers wish for anything else but the immediate and non-permanent gratification of its daily viewership. They would not pretend to be creating "Chekov."

Although initial instincts can be useful, more often than not there are depths to explore in a well-written text, which takes time and thoughtful investigation. So, we need a way in that will eschew the obvious or the cliché and allow us to begin to explore the specific ideas and emotional truths that are present in the text, in order to build our own unique interpretation.

Table Work

Many directors spend some time "around the table" doing script work at the beginning of a rehearsal process. I like to spend at least a week — if not ten days — on this phase. I wish I had longer. Traditional rehearsal processes, at least in Canada, are ridiculously short — between three and three-and-a-half weeks on average — and spending a week sitting around the table can seem counterintuitive at best, and downright irresponsible at worst.

But I have found that by engaging in a structured, provocative process of communal discovery, this work can start a cast of actors off on a much more interesting footing: bringing up myriad areas to explore, revealing the story, and identifying each character's role within it. Most importantly, we are building a common vocabulary to get everybody in the same play. It also usually saves time when beginning the process of staging, because much of the action has been discussed and begun to be investigated, and therefore much of the movement can be a direct result of the content already examined, instead of actors flailing about creating random pictures on the stage.

So, what is this way in?

What follows is a structure of how I've been mostly working for the past four-and-a-half decades. Others I have worked with have taken the basic structure and adapted it according to their own instincts. That's fine by me. It's offered here to be used or adapted as needed. If I am acting and the director works on their own text process — if they use one at all — I will still use this method for myself. Additionally, I have found it particularly helpful in new play workshops as a way of helping the playwright examine their script, without having the cast turn into a bunch of story editors. Much more on that in Chapter 14.

If the text is a forest, we need to identify specific trees to find our path. If the text is a woven garment, we need to examine individual strands to unravel its mysteries. If the text is a puzzle, we need to undo the finished picture and put it back together, perhaps even in a different way, recognizing that each piece is integral to the whole, and that certain ones may hold keys to fascinating, unique and unlooked-for possibilities.

Words are these trees, these strands, these pieces of the puzzle. In these treasures lie all we need to explore the worlds we hope to create on stage.

2

Getting Started

In what is often labelled a Stanislavskian method of text analysis, the dialogue is broken down into "beats of action." The actor is asked to "name" their action: the actor looks at their lines of dialogue and decides, "I'm browbeating them," or "I'm avoiding confrontation." They are asked what their objectives are in a scene, what their subtext is, and perhaps what their "super objective" is. All potentially valuable information, but in my opinion, way too early in the investigative process to discern, or worse, decide on, or worse still, choose a way of playing the moment before the explorative process has been allowed to gestate.

Additionally, this is a method that applies to naturalistic works almost exclusively more than other styles, since it is based primarily on the inner psychology of the characters and their interactions with each other. It asks that the puzzle be solved **before** the rehearsal work truly begins. I have always felt that whenever I worked this way as an actor, my answer to at least 90% of these questions was, "I don't know yet."

And yet I totally believe in text work before "getting on one's feet." I find that if actors are asked to investigate too much all at once: moving in space, exploring subtext and intention and backstory, and at the same time trying to relate to their fellow actors — most often with their scripts in hand — a certain amount of this chaos actually becomes entrenched, and not in a good way (although there are times when chaos can be invaluable). Decisions can either be left too late, or the messiness may be actually rehearsed until it becomes set, like an ill-formed piece of clay that is left too long after being quickly thrown on the wheel, without considered thought or examined purpose.

Worse yet is that if the text is not explored together with the complete cast, there will be a whole bunch of individuals doing whatever homework they might do, if any, and making choices that may or may not be germane to the story, and that their fellow castmates are not privy to. I have acted in way too many productions where the cast is asking questions of themselves in a vacuum — what's really going on here and why is it important to our play and why am I saying this thing right now? — way too late in the process, which could have saved time, not to mention confusion or frustration if done earlier and most importantly, together.

Now, I would never presume that all approaches should be the same no matter what the nature of the material. Different pieces may demand different approaches. But in every case, I have found that the following exercises help the actors find their "way in," no matter what the style of writing or presentation.

The First Read

The dreaded first read. Traditionally, this happens first in front of staff and crew and the design team. Most actors and directors hate them. Actors are nervous to be "performing" before they've even started rehearsals. Directors are hearing their cast all together, usually for the first time, and are praying that their choices in casting were sound. Designers are usually thinking about all the work there is to do and if they will have anywhere near the time and the resources they need to accomplish even a portion of their vision. The artistic director or producer is hoping that this group will come up with the goods and that the theatre won't go bankrupt. Of course, if it is a new play and the playwright is present, they are simply freaking out.

So, I submit that this is not part of the rehearsal process in any way. It is an anomaly; a false start. It's no use telling actors "not to perform" for this first read. They will either ignore you or take it so far in that direction as to be excruciatingly flat and "neutral" — a word, by the way, which actually has no meaning in the context of acting. Unless you can avoid it, the first read is something that must be endured and forgotten as soon as possible. Unless, of course, something interesting does emerge, because it occasionally does. Not often, but it does.

So, once the coffee and doughnuts have been shared and introductions made and the artistic director has welcomed us all and the read is finished and maybe even the set and costume designers have done their "show and tell," we can begin.

The Real First Read

So, everyone has left. It's just the actors, director, playwright (if applicable), and stage manager.

Let's start reading. But really reading.

Every mark on the page is part of the puzzle.

You might want to make a photocopy of the following text, as we will be referring to it a lot. It is a page of dialogue from the play *Lion in the Streets* by Judith Thompson, first produced in 1990 in Toronto at the World Stage Festival and the Tarragon Theatre. When I directed it in 2008, I was consistently moved by its powerful, poetic and idiosyncratic muscularity.

> *SUE rushes in, dressed in her sweat suit and sneakers.*
>
> *Everyone turns and freezes, except BILL, who continues to talk until SUE's third "Bill."*

SUE: Bill... Bill... Bill!! We have to talk!

BILL: Sue! Hi! Who's with the boys?

SUE: Mum came over, Bill I need to talk, NOW.

LAURA: Would you like a drink, Sue? We have...

GEORGE: Yeah, come in and sit down...

SUE: No, no thank you, I just... want to talk to my husband.

ISOBEL: My helper, Suuuuusan!

BILL: Oh — okay, Sue, I'll just finish this conversation. Anyway —

SUE: He thinks he's going to die.

BILL: Who?

SUE: Timmy! Your son! He —

BILL: What, did he say that tonight? Oh, that's just kids, he's —

SUE: BILL, come home, your son is very depressed his father is never there, why are you never never...

BILL: Sue PLEASE, we'll talk about it later, okay? So as I was saying, Laura...

SUE: Come with me.

BILL: I'll come in a while. I'll just finish this conversation, and then I'll come, okay?

SUE: YOU COME WITH ME NOW!

BILL: Sue.

SUE: Bill, I need you, please, why won't you come?

BILL: Why won't I come? Why won't I come? Because... (*he walks over to the others*) I'm... not.... I am not coming home tonight.

The play has a "La Ronde" structure, in that one of the characters in a scene then moves on to the next, interacts with another character, who in turn moves on to interact with another, etc. Isobel is the exception. She's the glue that binds the whole piece together and is the only character to address the audience. There is another character in this scene named Lily, who doesn't speak in this excerpt, and who we find out later is having an affair with Bill.

You will notice that Judith's writing is not "naturalistic." It might be called "magic realism" or "heightened naturalism" or any other label that is really useful only to academics rather than practitioners. The point is that Judith is not necessarily looking for lifelikeness in her work. Her writing is more stylized than that, revealing larger truths from a more enhanced version of reality than pure naturalism.

So, when we start the first real read, we break it down into "beats."

What Is a Beat?

In many ways, it is a purely arbitrary division. It is useful primarily to break the text down into manageable, bite-sized pieces to parse and discuss. I usually think in terms of action, or subject matter. For instance: in the above text, the beat would begin with Sue's entrance and go to Bill's line, "Oh — okay Sue, I'll just finish this conversation." It shouldn't include the next word, "Anyway," since I think that word starts the next beat. By the way, I should note here that Isobel is a ghost character who observes the action of the play and whom no one else can see or hear.

So, we have our beat. We should label it, with a scene number and beat letter. Although Judith did not feel the need to number her scenes in this play, I find that by doing so, it helps break the story down into component parts and highlights the narrative structure. This scene is the third one in the first act, after a "prologue" and two other scenes. It's actually the second beat of the scene, so this beat would be Scene 3 Beat b, or just 3b.

Stage Directions

The next step is to read it, including stage directions. I get the actors to claim their own stage directions by speaking them in the first person. For example, the actor playing Sue speaks, "I rush in, wearing my sweat suit and sneakers." It is important the actor read the direction exactly as written, except for changing the pronouns. This makes the stage direction an equal part of the character's text and must be given the same due as their dialogue. As the director, I will read the stage directions that are "directorial," such as, "Evening. The Jones' living room," and the like, as they don't belong to any character *per se*.

Why do this? Every good playwright chooses stage directions extremely carefully. They do not add them lightly. They are mostly included to make something clearer, or because they feel that something in the action is vitally important for the actor to know. In that one stage direction, the actor playing Sue has to acknowledge that she "rushes" into the scene. What does that mean? How does Sue "rush"? This is her third (and last) scene in the play. What happens in her previous scenes that initiate her rushing into this one? And why the indication of what she's wearing? Was she wearing the same outfit in the previous scenes? What does it say about her that she is wearing these clothes and rushing into this dinner party at her neighbour's house where her husband is…without her?

All of this, and more, from one sentence of stage direction.

I was once working on a monologue as an actor in rehearsal with a director and grappling with some complicated and very specific stage directions in the text. I asked the director what they thought a certain stage direction meant and why the playwright had felt the need to include it at this moment. The director replied that I should ignore it, and when I worked as a director, didn't I just cross out or otherwise discount the stage directions? I replied that on the contrary, I didn't, and that I always try to figure out what it has to tell me about how to interpret the text. To not take the stage directions seriously is disrespectful to the playwright. The director didn't know how to respond, never mind offer anything helpful to my original question.

So, I was left to my own devices to try to figure out why these stage directions were included. But it probably would have been more informative — and perhaps more fun — to do so in collaboration with the director and the rest of the cast.

Next, George, Laura, and Lily all say, "I turn and freeze." They can say it together or separately. Then Bill says, "Except me, and I continue to talk until Sue's third 'Bill.'" Finally, we get to Sue's first line of dialogue in the beat. Bill should begin to time his dialogue from the previous beat so that he is still talking over Sue's three "Bill"s.

Punctuation

In the same way that stage directions need to be exact, so too does punctuation. Most every playwright is very demanding that punctuation be acknowledged as integral to the dialogue. Judith is a prime example. She is not prescriptive about *how* the punctuation is necessarily spoken, just that it be taken into account.

For instance, exclamation points! What is the difference between one and several? Is it volume? Emphasis? And why sometimes are emphasized words CAPITALIZED, or *italicized*, or **bold**? Is there a difference between these choices? And why does Judith elongate certain letters, repeating them? For instance, later in this same scene, after a phone sex scene is re-enacted between Bill and Lily, Sue says, "BILLLLLLLLLLLLLLLLLLLLL!!!!!!!" followed by the stage direction, "*She physically attacks LILY.*" Before you count, I can tell you that there are eighteen L's after the two that are already in the name, and seven exclamation points. So, what is that? A wail? A roar? A growled whisper? A war-cry?

It could be any one of the above and more. At the beginning of rehearsals, the choice is not important. The recognition and engagement with the information is.

O O O

Some playwrights are extremely creative with punctuation. Kat Sandler, for instance, is fascinated by dialogue that overlaps or is spoken simultaneously by several characters. She writes: "A slash mark (/) marks the point in a character's line where the next character begins speaking. An asterisk (*) at the end of a line indicates the cue for a character to speak who has an * at the beginning of the line, even though a line or more of dialogue may separate the text of first character from the response of the other, or an indicator for a character to keep speaking OVER the character whose line separates their lines. An ellipsis (…) does not necessarily denote a long pause or a trail-off, more often a character searching quickly for a thought — think of them as short breaths or hesitations rather than dramatic pauses. If a line appears in (brackets) it means that line is tucked in/said under the lines around it."

George F. Walker often will put a period instead of a question mark at the end of a line which is clearly a question. Other playwrights won't use any punctuation at all.

The standard practice has been that a dash (—) at the end of a line means that the next line of dialogue interrupts the line, as opposed to ellipses (…) which is more of a trail off, but as you can read in Kat's piece above, these assumptions are changing.

O O O

I think of punctuation as a form of musical notation provided by a composer. Judith is also an actor, and I presume she hears the dialogue she writes in her head, as many playwrights do. In another instance, the third line of dialogue in the beat is Sue's line, "Mum came over, Bill I need to talk, NOW." No period after "Bill," or "over," which would be grammatically correct. (By the way, grammar and its rules are totally irrelevant in the creation of dialogue.) And there is a comma before the "NOW." Is that a set-up for hitting the capitalized word hard? Or not? Maybe it's more effective to emphasize with a small beat before speaking the word rather than volume? Or by over-enunciation? Or not.

So why does Sue speak the sentence that way? Are her thoughts tumbling out, one after another? Is there an overarching sense of urgency in needing to talk to Bill? Is she more emotional than rational at this point? Therefore, punctuation is not only a clue for how a line of dialogue may be delivered but may also be a signpost for meaning and intention.

Questions, Not Answers

Again, the choice at this point is not the issue. This phase of text work is just about gathering all the clues we can and identifying them to be considered by all the participants. It is about asking questions of your actors. And yourself.

A former brilliant teacher at the National Theatre School of Canada, Michael Mawson, gave me the best advice about directing I ever received. I was directing him in a workshop of a new work when I was a very young director. The day was over, and he was the last to leave. Just as he was walking out the door, he turned back and said, "You're a bright kid. You've got lots of answers to some really difficult questions. But it's not about the answers you have. It's about the questions you ask." And then he left.

So, after reading the beat, including stage directions, the questions begin, led by the director, with the whole group present. These are starting points for discussions. Again, the answer might be, "I don't know yet." Or they might have several possible answers to the questions.

And there are a lot of questions. They could be about their character, or their relationships with other characters, or their backstory, or large themes in the play, or small details, or anything else. Ask the actors playing the corresponding character/s these or similar questions:

1. Why is Bill there without Sue?

2. How long have they been married?

3. Are there more than two boys in their family? How old is the other boy? What's his name?

4. Why is it so important that Sue is dressed in a sweat suit and sneakers?

4. Why does everyone except Bill stop talking, and it takes three "Bill"s for him to finally stop?

5. Why do they freeze?

6. What was Laura going to say after "We have..."? What's in those ellipses?

Same with George's next line.

7. Do George and Laura know about Bill's affair with Lily?

8. Where did Bill and Lily meet?

9. What's in Sue's ellipses in her line "I just... want to talk to my husband."?

10. Why does Isobel have five "u's" in "Suuuuusan"?

And I have a lot more. I'm sure you might as well.

I then encourage the actors to ask *their* questions, if any. I NEVER ANSWER these questions, unless it is about an obvious fact that is answered somewhere else in the text. If an actor asks, "What is that about?" my only really useful reply is, "What do you think?" If they then say, "I don't know," my reply would most likely be, "Okay. Let's find out together. What are some of the possibilities?" Again, the exception to this would be if there is an obvious answer about something factual which is clearly stated somewhere else in the text, such as their age, or some other information. However, if that information comes from another character, it could be that that character either doesn't really know or is lying. Just two other possibilities.

So, we've identified the beat. We've read it, including stage directions. We've asked questions: about the punctuation, the subtext, the backstory, the characters' interactions, the character's costume (since it was seen fit to include it by the playwright), and anything else that deserves a question.

Why Do This?

It is imperative that every actor is part of these discussions, and that nothing falls between the cracks. We want as much information as possible to be gathered, investigated, discussed, and brought forward so that the actors have a wellspring of material to draw upon as they begin their work. Additionally, questions arising from the text are often just addressed with the individual actors as they work on their individual scenes, if they are addressed at all, and an opportunity for connections between what the other actors are dealing with just doesn't happen. This is a collaborative art form. Every participant should know as much as possible. There should be no secrets, nothing hidden from anyone.

By collectively discussing, asking questions, and exploring possibilities, all the actors can take ownership of the play and the story as a whole, and not just their part of it. They get to discover their role in the show, literally. And everyone else knows what that role is as well, in addition to their own. There also might be information that will have resonance for their character, or for another scene that they're in.

By the end of this process, we should all be able to answer the question "What is this play about?" in a concise, articulate and clear manner. We should all also be able to posit why it is important to present it. For me, there must be an urgency as to why I'm involved in a work of theatre. There has to be a burning imperative that demands communicating to the public. Otherwise, why subject oneself to the long hours, high stress, and small pay?

A production of a piece of theatre is one work. It is a sum of many contributions. Therefore, everyone has a stake in every word, not just their own. That said, actors can be very possessive about their characters. Rightly so. It might not be helpful or advisable to have other actors participate too much in the discussion about a character they're not playing, unless they are directly interacting with that character in a given moment. There is a delicate balance between inclusive discussion and another actor barging in on another's turf. And it is totally inappropriate for another actor to be prescriptive or to give notes to another actor. The director here must be a watchful and sensitive referee.

Now we get to pick words.

3

The Operative Word

Choosing Words

After the questions from that beat have been asked, I ask the actors to pick ONE word, and one word only, from their text in that beat — including their stage directions — that sums up that beat from their character's point of view. In a sense, it is their name for that beat. The word has to be from the dialogue they speak or a stage direction which applies to them.

What we are often looking for here is resonance — words that may have a greater meaning other than the surface obvious one. I almost always think that it's best that the word be a noun, verb, adjective or adverb.

It must be in the form as it appears in the text. For example, if the actor chooses the word "speaking," it should not be changed to "speak" or "speaks." The word can also include punctuation, if it immediately follows that word, such as an exclamation point or a question mark. Hyphenated words count as one word. Proper nouns, such as names of other characters or places, are discouraged. There are almost always more interesting choices. Exclamations, such as "wow" or "Yes!" are also discouraged, but exceptions can always be made under certain circumstances.

> My son Will, who used to teach English as a Second Language, tells me that nouns, verbs, adjectives and adverbs are called "content words" in the ESL field. Articles, prepositions, conjunctions and exclamations are labelled "function words." Content is generally much more useful in the choice of operative words than function.

Let's go back to our Beat 3b.

For Sue, it might very well be the word "talk," perhaps with an exclamation mark as it appears at the end of her first line. But it is important for the actor playing the part to choose. Maybe "rushes" is more to her liking, or "husband," or even "NOW." The choice is instinctive but considered. It might be discussed if appropriate. And of course, it can always be changed later.

All the actors in the scene get to choose a word. For the sake of this, I will say that:

> Bill chooses "conversation." "Continues" is also good.
> Both George and Laura choose "freezes."
> Lily chooses "turns."
> Isobel chooses "helper."

The actors write their word choices somewhere within the beat. They don't need to write anyone else's words, just their own.

Then, after all the actors have chosen, the director picks their own word to name the beat. It could come from anyone's text or stage direction, so that is why they choose last. I try to choose a word that is "directorial," in that it might describe the setting, or the overall feel of the beat, or from a directorial stage direction. I also try to choose one that has not already been picked. In this case, I'm going with "everyone," to emphasize the public nature of this horrific scene.

I always have a good dictionary on hand — either a Webster's or an Oxford English Dictionary — for the actors and myself to refer to. To help get at specificity, it is helpful to go to the dictionary to look for the etymology of certain words, and to check on the original and "true" meaning of the word, instead of an assumed one. Any word that seems provocative (from the Latin "to call forth") in any way can be looked up. Often actors will just begin doing this on their own after a while, intrigued by a certain word and wanting to know more of its origin and specific definition.

When looking at words with resonance, it's hard to top the word "conversation," especially in the context of this scene. It's from the Latin "to live with." There are many archaic and obsolete meanings of the word, such as a euphemism for sexual intercourse, a description of conduct or behaviour, as well as a "reversal of order" — all germane to Bill in this scene. Therefore, it's a pretty fantastic choice as an operative word. It opens doors. It doesn't shut any of them.

By the way, the word "resonance" comes from the Latin, literally "resound," or sound again, or echo. So, the resonance of a word can mean that it echoes in different ways and in different situations, giving it greater significance than simply its first hearing.

After the actors have written down their words and all of the choices have been noted by the stage manager, we move on to Beat 3c. It starts from Bill's "Anyway — " and continues for about 6 lines, up to and including Bill's line "Sue PLEASE, we'll talk about it later, okay?" but not the next part of his line.

Again, questions are asked, such as:

1.   How was this dinner party set up?

2.   Why is Sue not there?

3.   Was she invited but refused?

4.   Does she like being with the boys?

5.   What does Bill do for a living? What is Sue's work?

6.   Why does Bill ask Sue if Timmy said he was going to die tonight?

7.   Is Bill really "never there"?

I could go on, but you get the idea.

Answers may conflict with another actor's thoughts. For instance, the Sue actor may say Bill is home maybe once or twice a week and goes on work trips every two or three weeks. The Bill actor says that he thinks that's too much. He believes that he's home four or five times a week, and only goes on work trips every two months or so. This is a good disagreement and needs no resolution. The two actors are responding to a "fact" from a totally emotional, subjective point of view, and their characters have different views of reality. One person's truth is not another's. In fact, it helps to build the conflict between them that they have different versions of their shared reality. The actors don't have to agree in the same way their characters don't.

So, we choose words for Beat 3c. For sake of argument:

>   Sue chooses "depressed."
>   Bill chooses "kids."

George, Laura, Lily and Isobel have no text. But they are on stage, so they get to choose words. The ones with text — including stage directions — choose first, then the others can choose any word, even if one of the actors with text have chosen it already. Again, they are choosing from their character's point of view. In this case:

>   George chooses "son."
>   Laura chooses "home."

Lily chooses "kids" (same as Bill — how big an issue is it for Lily?)
Isobel chooses "die."
The director chooses "tonight."

Once again, these words have resonance. For Sue, who's really the one who is depressed? For Bill, if he's already thinking about leaving Sue, are his children part of his decision? Is he already thinking about custody, child support, and alimony, not to mention the emotional fallout for the boys? Does he feel any guilt whatsoever? Or none?

On to Beat 3d, and the process is repeated. This beat goes to the end of our example.

Questions:

1. How is each of the others reacting to this embarrassing exchange?

2. Does Lily know that Bill is "not coming home tonight"?

3. How much do George and Laura know about Bill's infidelity?

4. Who invited Lily?

5. Has Lily ever seen Sue before?

6. How does Lily feel about Sue's physical appearance?

7. Had Bill thought that tonight would be the night he'd end his marriage? In fact, is that what he's doing?

8. What's Isobel thinking/feeling/doing during all this?

Again, there are many more than this. Often, the questions begin great conversations. However, it's important that the discussions not get bogged down in too much detail but remain open to options and potential playable intentions.

Again, for illustration, I will say that:

> Sue chooses "need."
> Bill chooses "finish."
> George says "home."
> Laura chooses "conversation."
> Lily chooses "come."
> Isobel picks "Why?."
> The director chooses "NOW."

This process continues for the whole play. You can possibly understand why it's easy to spend a whole week working on the text around the table in this manner.

Why Do This?

> I directed my daughter Natasha in a workshop several years ago, and started working on the text using this system. I could see her reacting badly as I introduced it. She writes, "I was trying to be cool, because you were my dad, and I wanted to be professional, but I didn't think much of the exercise at first. I'd done a bunch of operative words stuff in school, mostly about what word you stress when you're acting, and I thought that was a bit silly. However, when the exercise switches gears, when it all comes together, it took me by surprise and I was floored."

Needless to say, this work has nothing to do with which word to stress.

Ultimately, what we're doing here is dividing the text into manageable pieces and each actor gets to name them for themselves, while being asked and asking some extremely relevant questions. We are trying to make sure that little or no information falls between the cracks. We are, in a sense, building the world and a shared vocabulary for the play. We're also parsing the narrative into practical portions in order to see how it's all constructed.

Again, it is vital that this work is done by all the actors together. Too often, after the dreaded first read-through, the company is split up to begin work on their scenes, even if they start by doing table work, and only the actors involved in that scene are called. Very often, the rest of the cast might view the other actors' work only at "stumble-throughs," and later, run-throughs. I will work this way in the next phase of rehearsal, when we start to stage the play after our communal text work. It is cruel and unusual punishment for the rest of the cast to witness the often painfully slow process of the first work-through on one's feet after the text exploration.

But this text work is the excavation phase. By doing this work together, every actor is in on the examination of the text: its themes, its subtext, and the reasons that make this story important. Everybody is participating in the investigation of the narrative, as well as each character's journey, and thereby the creation of our interpretation of the story.

Equally important, each actor is taking ownership of each beat that they're in and giving it a name that is theirs and theirs alone. They're choosing their words from their character's point of view. They are not being asked to make any decisions about how those words are played, nor invent any language other than the one that is already written by the playwright. In this way, it is a supremely non-judgmental exercise using an entirely instinctive process. The choices often tend to be emotional rather than intellectual, which is a very good thing at this early stage of rehearsals. The actors are beginning to understand their character's inner life, to be an advocate for their character, to understand their character's *raison d'être*, and to investigate how their character interacts with the other characters in each scene and throughout the whole play.

These choices are specific and are building a narrative vocabulary that everyone in the process is privy to. When someone says one of their operative words, it's like a code that only this team understands. Besides being a great tool for cast bonding, we are also building listening habits. And there can never be too much listening between actors.

Another Note about Specificity

The work of the interpretive artist is to unearth and reveal specificity. If you attempt to create art that is *trying* to be universal, you will inevitably veer towards cliché. As a species, we respond most strongly to a specific tale, told in unique ways, as a way to empathy and understanding.

> When Ted Dykstra and I wrote *2 Pianos 4 Hands*, we were convinced that it was only going to speak to piano nerds, or at best, classical music nerds. After our first workshop presentation, our old friend Andrew Akman came up to us and said, "The play's not about the piano at all. It's about tennis." Andrew had been a promising young tennis player in Winnipeg as a teenager, and he related every scene from our play to his experience. When Ted said to me as one of my teachers in the play, "You're not Glenn Gould!", Andrew heard, "You're not John McEnroe!", something that had been said to him by a teacher at a similar juncture in his life.

Specificity, like so many other worthwhile endeavours, is a bottomless pit. We don't know what will ultimately speak the strongest to an audience or any member of it. But we do know that any chance of real, significant communication must be rigorously specific in order to have even a chance to speak to the many.

Language as a whole, and individual words in particular, lose specificity from overuse, or appropriation, or incorrect application. We all make assumptions. A lot.

O O O

If I say the word "entertainment" to you, what do you see? Close your eyes and let your imagination roam. Most people talk about a Broadway show, a movie musical, a Super Bowl halftime show starring a well-known pop star, or even an interactive video game. There might even be a slightly dismissive judgment of these imaginings, as in "it's only entertainment" — as opposed to deep, complex drama, perhaps. However, the word comes from a Latin root: *enter* means between, and "tain" comes from *tenere*, meaning "to hold." So, the original meaning of the word means "to hold between," presumably interest between a performer and their audience. And yet, we have all these assumptions, preconceptions and clichéd images about the word — and even a judgment about its definition! Blame the mass media, our fast-paced life, or a conspiracy of the Freemasons, but language is constantly in a state of reductivism. This is not necessarily a bad thing, although many decry the death of interesting verbal dexterity and debate. But these assumptions must be taken into account, since most people don't obsessively look for specificity in their day-to-day communications. But theatre artists must.

O O O

So. The story is slowly being revealed. As the questions are asked and discussed, and as the operative words are chosen, all manner of narrative content is uncovered, and within the context of an exercise. What's important about this is that there is a focus to the discussion, instead of a free-for-all, where often only the loudest voices in the room are heard, and where the discussion can lack a structural and forward thrust. And hopefully, nothing is left unexamined.

Every Character Gets a Voice

Every character gets a word to name the beat, whether or not they even speak or have a stage direction in that beat. As long as they are on stage, the beat has a name for them, and they get to choose that name. They are contributing to the discussion and to the discovery of the narrative in as major a way as any other actor. The protagonist and the smallest character have equal status here, *as long as they are on stage.* How fascinating to hear what a wordless attendant might be thinking and feeling about the actions and dialogue they are witnessing. How great that they are able to build three-dimensional, complex characters, whether or not they speak from the stage.

I make sure to solicit this discussion from everyone, especially those who are playing the smallest parts (they tend to be the youngest) and most especially if they feel intimidated by the more experienced ones in the room. It's imperative to check in with these younger, often softer voices, to make sure that they are heard and that they are given the same respect as the actors playing the leads. The play may not be their story, but every actor has a significant role to play in its telling.

As previously stated, my choice of word as the director often tries to encapsulate the beat from an "objective" point of view, describing a location, time, subject matter, or some other factor. However, it hopefully can also be a provocative spur, and I will often pick a word that is meant to incite a reaction from one or more of the characters.

An example of this might be in the Beat 3d where I chose "NOW," especially as it is also capitalized in the text. When I describe the exercises that follow, I will show how that provocation can function.

Story

There are lots of ways story or narrative has been analyzed and divided into sections: the three-act structure often cited in TV or film scripts, Shakespeare's five-act structure, Chekov's four acts, etc. Some artists hate these limitations, and are actively searching for alternative narrative models, or wish to have no model at all.

When dealing with relatively traditional narratives, I will sometimes use the classic Aristotelian structure — five sections divided as such:

> Part 1 — Introduction
> Part 2 — Development
> Part 3 — Climax
> Part 4 — Denouement
> Part 5 — Resolution

Most people are surprised that the climax is number 3, instead of appearing later. Climax here is defined as the event that irreparably changes the world of the characters. What we often refer to as the climax (whose etymological root comes from the Greek word for "ladder") is the emotional or action-based height of the story, where the protagonist is at the height of their conflict or dilemma, usually found towards the end of Part 4 of the narrative structure cited above. However, by identifying the climax as defined as the event that changes our world, each actor can experience this event from their own point of view, with their own reactions to it, and perhaps their own emotional climax.

Discussing together how the narrative is structured helps the actors understand where they are in their own individual journeys and how that journey relates to the other characters. When this work is done alone — if it is done at all — by the director in isolation, this knowledge becomes like a magic key that only they or perhaps a select few have access to. But when the narrative is discovered by everyone together, we are all able to delineate the larger trees through the forest and bring our story to light.

Often actors can get overwhelmed by the amount of text they may have. They are challenged as to know how to begin, especially when playing a large part with lots of words. How does one start to navigate all the choices that eventually need to be made?

Instinct is good, but it can only carry one so far without some sense of methodology. First ideas are useful but may be limiting. "Winging it" can be helpful and sometimes exciting, but there might be much more to the play than meets the eye, never mind the ear, brain and gut.

Structure can often be liberating. It provides a base from which to fly. Not having a structure can give the illusion of freedom, but often leaves the actor flopping on the beach, like a fish desperately trying to regain the water to swim its way back to where it can breathe and live.

Again, this method is a non-judgmental way of breaking down the whole. It opens doors, offers options, and demands no early decisions. It is a way to reveal the essential narrative. Each actor is building the journey of their character, and this process allows for discovering a path to navigate this journey. It's not intellectual, but there is a good deal of thinking required. There is mystery, but not for its own sake. It's instinctive, but it is all rooted in the text — the words that are actually there, written by the author. We're not making anything up. We're just excavating what the playwright has given us.

Different Styles, Different Questions, Same Words

So even though Judith Thompson's play is not "naturalistic," but rather some heightened form of realism, this method helps in anchoring what is going on in the text. Some scripts may care less about psychology, backstory, or subtext. They may be more image-based, or abstract, or absurd, or fantastical.

This method is useful in those texts as well. Even though the text may not be asking the actor to delve into the inner psychology of their character, that does not mean there is no mooring that can help them in their investigation. Indeed, the conflict between "reality" and the non-realism of the world created by the writer may be the very stuff of what makes the work compelling. In *Lion in the Streets,* Isobel, our protagonist, is a ghost who is on a quest —for peace, for vengeance, for understanding, for grace. This is not naturalism, but for Isobel and us, the audience, it is a real and urgent journey. The actor playing the part, the director, and the cast that is on stage with her can piece together this mission of hers on its own terms, with its own set of rules of its *theatrical* reality.

Most actors need some baseline from which to play. Call it history, or intention, or context, but it is impossible to act a style of performance or writing. The questions one asks as a director may be different, and have less to do with some traditional elements in more naturalistic scripts, but the specificity of the exploration is still invaluable in providing a foothold for the actor to begin to get at something that is playable and concrete, as opposed to an amorphous intellectual concept or a version of reality that is purely theoretical. The parameters might be different — more abstract or imagistic — but there are still parameters that create our theatrical construct.

Because the method is non-judgmental, in that the performer is not making up any choice of their operative word than what appears in the text, or that they're not being asked to make judgments about what their character is *really* feeling or doing in a given passage, the process works equally well for a diversity of pieces portrayed in a wide variety of ways.

Similarly, story can be parsed even in — or perhaps especially in — a non-traditional, non-linear narrative. It may not be obvious or clear what that tale is, but there is always a story present that needs delineating.

Stories are, after all, the basis of all performative communication. When all is said and done, theatre artists are simply storytellers.

4

The Exercises

Exercise #1 — The Read-through... Again

So, all the beats have been delineated. A lot of questions have been asked, and there may be lots more. Lots of discussion about themes and characters and words and relationships and all kinds of other issues arising from our play have been had. And all the operative words have been chosen for the whole play. This has all taken at least several days, if not a week. Now what?

We do another read-through. But this time, we read just the operative words.

First, get the actors to write their words opposite the scene and beat number as a list for the whole play. For example, the actor playing Sue would write, when we got to this scene and beat:

> 3b — talk!
> 3c — depressed
> 3d — need

All the actors and the director do this for their own words (they don't need to notate anyone else's but their own). It is important that everyone is clear which scene and beat each word belongs to. The stage manager should have all the information about that and be ready to clear up any confusion. It is also important for the actors to list the scene numbers and beat letters of those they are not in and leave them blank. It is valuable information to know when (and perhaps why) you're not onstage at any point in the narrative.

In the case of actors playing more than one part in a play, it is important to keep the chronology of the play as a whole in mind, as well as when they play which character. So, they would list the scene/beat numbers in order, but make sure they know when they're a different character. There are really two narratives going on: the play's story, in which all the characters participate, and each character's story, which is as complete and complex no matter how much text is devoted to their existence.

Often, actors, having gotten better at choosing stronger, more interesting words as the process has gone on, will want to change their word choice. Totally kosher. I'll even have actors tell me during the run, or even after the show has closed, that they've changed their word choices.

Over time, I have discovered that this read-through of the operative words works best when there are certain rules that are adhered to:

1) Each beat is introduced by the director with the scene and beat number. For example, I would say when we got to this point, "Scene 3, Beat b." As this reading goes along, I often just say, "3b."

2) There should be no speaking of any kind other than this text, i.e., the director's introduction, and the participants' words. Absolutely none. No comments. No discussions. Nada.

3) Each participant, including the director, MUST say their word. They cannot choose to abstain.

4) Each participant, including the director, may NOT say their word more than three times. Therefore, after the director speaks the scene/beat number, each participant can say their words once, twice or three times. No more than thrice, no less than once.

5) There is no pre-arranged order as to when each participant speaks their words. I ask the participants to look at their word after the scene/beat number has been called, "memorize" it, and make eye contact with the others. When it feels right, jump in with your word. If it feels like your word initiates something in this beat, go for it. If not, don't. If it feels right to answer another character's word with your own, do so. You may end up saying your word three times in a row at some point. That's fine, but remember, that's it. You've used your quota for that beat. You may say it once to no one in particular, or to a specific character, or to everyone. That's fine, too, as long as you say it.

6) How you say your word is up to you in that moment. Eye contact is vital, even if it may not be once the beat is staged. You can imbue your word with all the meaning/emotion/ urgency that seems appropriate. If you've chosen to include punctuation, take that into account. This is both a read-through and a quasi-improvisation.

The director is the chair of this process, deciding when to move on to the next beat, and if there is a pace that is naturally building, that may be taken advantage of. As mentioned earlier, I often find that as the director, I can act as somewhat of an *agent provocateur*, challenging one or more characters with my choice of words and how I say it. For instance, if my choice is "NOW" as it was for Scene 3d in our example, I might challenge one or more of the characters with it, such as Bill or Lily or Sue or George or all four by using my word "NOW" to try to force them to act or speak, putting pressure on them in an already pretty tense situation.

What results from this read-through is often surprising. For a start, the story usually reveals itself quite clearly, even though the text is so stripped down. Because there has been a decent amount of discussion about each beat, and each word choice by each actor has been chosen with the rest of the participants in attendance, the words take on the resonance and context of the story. Each of the chosen words is precious, since they can only be spoken three times, so the actor truly gives each utterance its due. But now the words take on the context of existing in relation to others' choices. Are there conflicts that the words heighten, and what are they really about? Are there allegiances between characters, and do they shift? Do certain words initiate action, or are they reactions to others' impulses?

The conflicts between characters are being explored, without overstating or endless discussion about subtext or psychology. The actors are working very hard to listen and to communicate with each other, even if their characters sometimes aren't. They are desperately trying to figure out where they are in the story and their own journey — which is just like life, no? Dialogue, in its truest sense, is being engaged, complete with eye contact, and with a pretty full sense of each character's agenda. Because the dialogue is only one word, there is no sense of them waiting for the other character/s to say their line/s in order for you to speak yours. They are truly LISTENING to each other, because they must in order to engage in the exercise. There is a fascinating interplay being developed between how the characters' journeys intersect against how steadfastly — or not — other characters are dealing with their own agendas.

It is always helpful after the whole read-through is finished to discuss what was learned or discovered by the exercise. Was the story clear? Were there dips and valleys in the narrative? Was there a clear point of climax? Did anyone get lost as to where we were? Did they find they were really trying to communicate to one character in particular? Was this reciprocated? Did they feel isolated? Or part of a group? Was their emotional journey urgent and clear, or confused? Were the story and its themes changed by this distillation?

Exercise #2 — The Monologue

Each actor reads their complete list of operative words for the whole play. They speak each word only once and separate them by at least a second or two. It is often helpful if the other actors close their eyes to listen. If the actor reading feels so inclined, the pace of their "character monologue" might increase and gather momentum and/or intensity as it goes along.

They should be strongly warned not to overact this monologue. This exercise is about the words and the journey they reveal, not the performance of them. In a large sense, the actor is the conduit for the words, as they (arguably) always should be. But again, it's too soon to start really acting. We're still just gathering information.

I find this exercise surprisingly emotional. By reducing a character's journey to individual words, a subtle yet palpable power is revealed that is unencumbered with other verbiage. This list of words is not about behaviour, but about the essence of the character's life for the period of this story. There is no conflict between the hidden and the revealed, the public and the private, the text and the subtext. The words take on a certain primal, elemental significance.

After each monologue, it can be interesting to discuss what everyone might have observed. Again, was the journey clear? Were there obvious peaks and valleys? Where was the climax for that character? Was there a grouping of the words in a given section that was illuminating? Is there a certain grammatical tendency, such as a preponderance of verbs or adjectives? Was it different from the play as a whole? Is there a picture of who this person is, revealed in much the same way that sculptors often describe a work emerging from the slab of stone?

Exercise #3 — Redux

Next, I like to reduce the number of words by choosing one of the words already chosen to encompass a larger section. In the case of *Lion in the Streets*, it's easy enough to break it down into scenes.

So, after the read-through of the whole play and the monologues, I ask the actors to choose a word that feels right for a whole scene; one word that might encompass the essence of that scene from their character's point of view. It's important that the word is selected from the ones already chosen and not some new one. If a new word is starting to rear up and say, "Choose me!", then change your word for the beat in which it appears.

Again, it's important that the words chosen are in the grammatical form and with any corresponding punctuation or typeface (italics, caps, etc.) as it appears in the text. Even changing those parameters is making a judgment that moves away from the text as written.

Then we do another read-through, using the same rules as Exercise #1. The director says the scene number, the actors memorize their word, make eye contact, and say their word when appropriate. As before, they must say it at least once, and no more than three times. Is the story still making sense? Are the relationships, conflicts, and character journeys becoming even more crystallized? Are we getting closer to the most elemental of the narrative's imperatives? Any other observations?

After the choice of one per scene, I reduce it further to a larger section. Perhaps one per five of our narrative sections, or any other delineation that may seem appropriate. Three acts, four or two. It doesn't totally matter, as long as it makes sense to all. Repeat the read-through.

Lastly, can we get it down to one word for each character for the whole play? Is there an absolute, essential word that sums up the play from each character's point of view, as well as the director's objective one? Again, repeat this very short read-through.

Then, we can take a moment to examine each actor's choice. Does it make sense in our new, evolving context? Does this word act as a doorway for exploration? Each actor should look up their word and share its etymology with the group, perhaps explaining why that word jumped up at them and seemed to say, "Choose me!" Did they have other words that were also vying for the position of Chief Operative Word?

Exercises #4 and Up — Working with the Words

There are many different ways to use the words, and now is the time when there can be a physical entry into the work. The table work so far has been sedentary — necessarily so — and pretty soon, if not already, the actors are champing at the bit to get on their feet. This is a valuable instinct.

Some of these exercises are dependent upon the group one is working with. As mentioned earlier, I would hesitate to use some or all of these exercises with seasoned professionals. Some of them are way more appropriate for acting students, or perhaps young professionals.

Operative words can be great clues for physicality.

I was directing *Nothing Sacred* by George F. Walker at the Vancouver Playhouse, and the wonderful actor Robert Clothier, best known as Relic in the classic Canadian TV series *The Beachcombers*, was in the cast. We did this exercise, and his operative word for the whole play was "foot." It came from his line, "I try to put one foot in front of me, but the other foot won't come with it." Using this word, Robert developed a physicality for the character that was absolutely delightful. Every time he started to exit, he would begin to leave in one direction, and change his mind and leave another way. He would go to sit in a chair and end up sitting in another. He could never make up his mind about the simplest and most mundane of actions, which of course was the psychology of his inner turmoil about larger issues in the play. It was a funny, charming, sad and revealing choice, and I'm sure that neither he nor I would have come up with this image without this work.

a — Psychological Gesture

This anecdote illustrates how the physical life of a character can be directly linked to one's inner emotional truth.

Too often, young actors see acting from the neck up only, no doubt a product of growing up watching endless hours of screen acting. The idea that an actor is encompassed with a whole body, where the size and style of performance may be "larger than life," where a world is created that is not necessarily a mimic of "reality," is an increasingly unfamiliar concept. And yet, still young hopefuls come to theatre schools to train. They somehow know that theatre acting is how you learn to act, and then you "graduate" to film and TV and the web, although later you may return to the theatre to "really challenge yourself and your craft." And of course, some fools actually fall in love with the theatre as a medium and devote their entire professional lives to it. Like me.

Using one or more of the operative words, the actor can begin to develop a physical vocabulary for their character. It's always good to start in a stylized manner, allowing the size of the exploration to be big, even grotesque. Giving the actor time and space alone, they are encouraged to explore what the word initiates physically to reveal the psychology of their character.

b — The Mini Solo Play

Using the operative word chosen for the whole play, the actor must enter, make eye contact with the audience, speak the word — accompanied with suitable gesture/s — three times, then exit.

I will often give the actors about fifteen minutes to rehearse this exercise on their own. I will often describe the gesture they are exploring as "psychological." How does the gesture or gestures illuminate the word?

Back to our example text: if the actor playing Sue chooses the word "depressed" from her beat 3c for the whole play, how does her body communicate this word? Again, etymology is helpful. It comes from the Latin *depressare*, meaning "to press down." Can she play with these concepts? Is she pressing down, or is she being pressed down, and if so, by whom? Is she fighting against it, or giving in to it?

A variation of this exercise is that the actor enters and speaks their character name in a manner as it appears in the play (e.g. "Suuuuusan!" as in our sample text), accompanied either by the same psychological gesture, or perhaps transformed into another. In a sense, the character's name becomes their text, and the operative word their subtext. Always limit the number of times of repetition to three. Again, the more a word is repeated, the less power it has. And what does the name mean? Can you find an etymological source for the name? Why did their parents (or the playwright) choose that name for them? How does their character feel about their name?

c — Tableaux

A great group exercise to get at the themes of the piece. The group stands in a circle, armed with their operative words. One of them says their word strongly and clearly. The next three to five participants to the left of the speaker rush into the centre, without talking, and quickly create a tableau, or three-dimensional sculpture as a reaction to the word. They must end up frozen and in physical contact with at least one of the other tableau makers. Every part of their body should be engaged, including their faces. They hold their positions while the other participants look at this "work of art" from all sides. After about thirty seconds or so, they can release and return to the circle. A short discussion might ensue. Then move on to the next person in the circle to speak their word, and the next tableau is created, adding the next person down the line.

I will also sometimes "animate" each tableau. As the group is frozen, ask that they make a sound suggested from their pose, and repeat it three times simultaneously with the rest of the participants. Then ask that they move to the next position that seems to suggest itself, together with everyone else. Make sure that they move only — without sound — and that they stay in contact with at least one other tableau participant by the end of their movement, even if it's a different person from the first image. Then add both movement and sound together, done three times, returning to the original position each time. The movement and sound should not be long — a couple of seconds in length at most. Again, discuss as appropriate, but often it's better to just leave the images to percolate without discussion.

d — The Lecture

A variation of the mini solo play: the actor must give a one- or two-minute lecture on their word. They can use etymology, or stream-of-consciousness associations, or anything else they wish as the content of their lecture. It's possible to add that they are hiding a physical condition that they do not want the audience to notice. For instance, if they are talking about "foot," their foot might have uncontrolled spasms which they try to cover up. If their word is depressed, they may be pressed down from time to time and try to normalize this somehow.

This is a *commedia dell'arte* kind of exercise, and thereby essentially comic. This is always a good thing, especially when the work is not particularly comic, as in *Lion in the Streets*. I have found that the opportunities of finding comedy in a drama are as important as making sure that a comedy is ALWAYS rooted in the real. Look for lightness in the dark and shadows in the brightness.

o o o

Alfred Lunt and Lynn Fontanne, the famous American husband and wife actor/managers, used to take hit shows that they had opened on Broadway on extended tours across the States. One night, during one such long run, as they were getting ready in their dressing room, Lunt said, "I don't know. Every time I used to ask for the tea, I used to get this large laugh. Now it's not there." Fontanne replied, "Well, darling, that's because you're asking for the laugh. Try asking for the tea."

o o o

Other Useful Exercises

The following can be used as homework for each actor only, with no need to share with the rest of the group:

1. Using your operative words, get the actors to make a list of five of the ones that have the most resonance for their characters — whether they were picked from the Redux Exercise or not — for their journeys. Why did they choose those five? What are their etymologies? What does it say about their character's backstory, or their psychological profile, or their self-esteem and place/status in the world? Are there any other issues or thoughts that spring from these words?

2. Another valuable exercise is one that stems from Stanislavski. Get each actor to make three lists. They are:

    • All the things your character says about yourself,

    • All the things your character says about others, and

    • All the things others say about your character.

3. Get the actors to write down questions they may have:

    • What do you find provocative about the story? About your character?

    • What are you dying to explore in playing this character?

    • Describe your character physically. Are they different from you? (see below)

    • What are the most striking images from the story about your character? About the whole story?

    • What role does the audience play in experiencing this story?

4. Another valuable tool, especially for theatre school students, is the Laban dynamics of movement. For those of you who don't know it, here is a simplified explanation:

The dynamics of movement have three factors: weight, speed and direction. Each of these has two variables — light or heavy for weight, fast or slow for speed, and direct or indirect for direction. Therefore, there are eight permutations and combinations of these factors, each of which has a name:

    1) Puncher (heavy, fast, direct)
    2) Slasher (heavy, fast, indirect)
    3) Presser (heavy, slow, direct)
    4) Wringer (heavy, slow, indirect)
    5) Dabber (light, fast, direct)
    6) Flicker (light, fast, indirect)
    7) Glider (light, slow, direct)
    8) Floater (light, slow, indirect)

Which one are you as a person? Which one is your character? Do your operative words suggest a choice?

All kinds of exercises can be created using these dynamics to facilitate the beginning of a physical characterization for the actor.

So. We've done our research. We've examined the text.

It's time to start creating our inimitable, unique and specific interpretation of it. It's time for context.

PART TWO

—

CONTEXT

5

What Is Directing?

Most of the best directing I do is providing *context* for others to do their best work.

The job of director is relatively new in the history of theatre, at least as it has evolved and been interpreted in the last hundred years or so. And yet the amount of authority and power that has been granted the position seems out of whack with what I believe to be the heart of its purpose.

Directors have somehow been granted the authority as the one AND ONLY purveyor of the artistic vision. Their word is sacrosanct. All ideas must stem and flow from them and — depending on exactly how much control they like to wield — no decisions can be made without their approval. Having worked under this system for many years, I must admit there is a seductive feeling of power in this structure. It's easy to get used to. But it is ultimately counter-productive.

To be sure, the director initiates major portions of the discussions — hopefully emanating from the text — with designers, actors, technicians, and producers, but having initiated these discussions, they should actively solicit input from their collaborators for them to take that impetus and add to it. The trick for the director is deciding whether or not what is being proposed is germane to the context. And even more importantly, being able to articulate why something is or is not part of the theatrical world that we are all trying to create together, in order to get the appropriate input from everyone.

Now of course, some things just boil down to taste. My taste may not be the same as one of my collaborators'. This is where the director's "final say" comes into play. But I would argue that you should try to resist using this power to decide too quickly on anything that has multiple options. These decisions should be discussed until the last possible, practical moment, and all attempts should be made to come to a consensus with your collaborators, unless, of course, there are deadlines that must be met sooner rather than later. After all, there might be other choices which could ultimately surprise you or turn out to be better in a totally unlooked-for way.

Why I Chose to Direct

I always knew I wanted to direct. I'm not sure why, but I think I felt comfortable leading without being dictatorial and striving to inspire and energize a group of artists.

I instinctively knew that to be a good director, I needed to be the best actor I could be. To be clear: I do not believe you HAVE to be an actor to direct, but I do believe that the heart of the position is being sympathetic to and understanding of the essence of acting. Lots of great directors were never actors or are long-retired actors. If a director is not (or never has been) an actor, their first course of study should be to learn what goes into the craft and art of this somewhat mysterious activity.

I don't think I was a "born actor," whatever that is. I wasn't good at impersonations or instant characterization. I wasn't totally comfortable with being on stage, although I was the "class clown" in school and I did do well performing as a young pianist in competitions and exams.

When I first began acting, I was extremely self-conscious about performing, being too objective and judgmental to be relaxed and available to an audience. The irony was that as I trained, which luckily enough for me was at the best and most innovative theatre school at the time — the Royal Academy of Dramatic Art in London, England — I actually fell in love with the challenge and complexity of acting. I learned invaluable skills that became indispensable to my directing: listening, being present, being emotionally accessible, being responsive to both my fellow actors and the audience, and the essence of storytelling. I still love to act.

But after graduating and becoming a professional actor, I quickly became frustrated when I observed directors in shows I was in floundering to express themselves, or not knowing how to rehearse, or not seeing the problems in front of them, never mind offering possible solutions. Some had interesting ideas but couldn't communicate effectively with actors or had no understanding of the actor's process. Others were good communicators, but without interesting ideas or informed choices. Some were better with designers than actors, and some the reverse. I worked with very few directors I found truly talented and inspiring in all areas.

There is certainly a pretty strict structure in the rehearsal room, and other actors are not generally encouraged to express their ideas in scenes in which they are not participants, unless specifically asked, or if the discussion is deliberately opened up to include the whole group. So, I very often couldn't contribute to the discussion. But I could watch rehearsals for which I was not called, or technical rehearsals when none of the actors were called, or overhear discussions between designers and directors. I would bite my tongue, internally screaming that the path forward seemed so obvious, but with no voice to express my ideas. I knew I had to direct.

When I went to theatre school, there were very few directing programs, and none that were part of a theatre school as opposed to a university. At that time, most directors who hadn't come from acting came from universities, especially in Britain where I trained.

I knew that for me, the last place to learn was at an institute of academic learning rather than a "trade school." Academic study and/or research is a means to an end which can be extraordinarily useful to theatre practitioners, but not an end in itself. Theatre is not theoretical. It is pragmatic in the extreme, both in its conception and its execution. Ideas and theories are useless if they are unplayable, or unrealizable due to them being too abstract or limited by live performance exigencies, such as time, money or resources.

So, I had to learn by doing it.

Experience

Like all trades or crafts, experience is the best teacher. In acting training, certain precepts and techniques can and should be taught, but unless the actor feels the truth of that lesson in their body, it is not truly incorporated (literally "form into a body"). The process is exactly the same for a director. Even though some techniques can be taught or you can assistant direct (see Chapter 8), it is impossible to teach communication skills without the practice of communicating to different people doing different jobs in different productions with different circumstances. The director has to communicate clearly, respectfully and honestly to everybody involved in the production, and find the right words or images that make sense to that individual. The permutations and combinations are as endless as the individuals with whom you're communicating.

So, what to do? Practise, practise, practise. As often as possible. Fringe Festivals, self-producing, little shows in church basements — anywhere, everywhere, and constantly — and while you're doing that and discovering your own process, make sure that it's inclusive, creative and fun, and practise applying it over and over, honing and adapting it to your aesthetic and the practicalities of each individual situation, each of which will have its own unique factors and circumstances. No play is the same, neither is each cast, each collaborator, each performance space, nor the state of the world at that particular moment in history. In creating theatre, we create a new and unique world — each and every time.

Adaptability, flexibility, acknowledging difficulties, and reacting to different and changing realities are the touchstones, while holding true to your impulses and your reasons for doing this piece in the first place. The saving grace is that there is a creative solution to every challenge. Problems are opportunities, and limitations can be seen as fortuitous. Theatre is the art form of pure imagination. This is its greatest resource and production value. Any obstacle can be overcome if we are imaginative enough to see our way through it.

Leadership

What qualities do you admire in a leader? Who were the most effective leaders you have encountered? What made you admire them, and want to follow them?

I want my cast and crew to feel confident. I want them to feel free to do their best work, and yet know that this art form is never easy. I want them to know that if they feel lost or confused about anything that they can ask me for help, and that I will be able to help them with an idea or image that will unblock the obstacle in their way. I want them to feel that I am sympathetic to their problems and yet confident in their abilities. I want them to feel like equal participants in a communal endeavour.

Never take yourself too seriously. Make fun of yourself, and give others the permission to make good-natured fun of you as well. Humour is an invaluable tool to put your collaborators at ease and to feel that everything and anything is possible and solvable.

The worst leaders are those that have to insist that they are to be respected and trusted. As my father used to say, "Never trust anyone who asks to be trusted." As always, you lead by example. Be the collaborator you would like to work with. Respecting others is the only way to gain their respect.

True leadership is earned. It can never be assumed by one's position in some hierarchical system. There is absolutely no reason for anyone to follow you unless by doing so, their own work will flourish.

6

Pre-Production

Casting

A most mysterious process.

I sometimes wish there was a more scientific method of picking actors than presently exists. But then there wouldn't be the mystery, would there? And it's the mystery that makes the art.

My late mother was an educational psychologist. She worked at a CEGEP in Montreal, and when I was at RADA in London in the early '70s, my parents came to visit me. She asked for a meeting with our principal, a brilliant man named Hugh Crutwell.

She asked Hugh how he went about choosing students for the program. He did all the auditions and callbacks himself, sometimes with others to solicit additional feedback, but he was known for having strong, and sometimes unusual, opinions about young people and their potential. At that time, he would accept twenty-one new students every intake, usually fourteen men and seven women (oh how times have changed), out of an average of one thousand applicants from around the world.

When my mother asked her question, he looked at her with a sort of bemused amazement, which I took as a judgment of how ridiculous he thought the question was. He said, "Pure instinct. That's all. What else do I possibly have?"

In my class alone, we had a fascinating array of diverse individuals, several of whom had never set foot upon a stage in their lives.

So, that's my method. Instinct.

Truth be told, there are many actors who could play any part you have in mind. In Canada, the unemployment rate for stage actors is about 90% at any given time, according to most sources, and that was pre-COVID! There are many more actors than there are parts, and many ways to make casting way more interesting than finding the "perfect actor for the part," whatever that means. But someone must be cast, so someone is chosen.

As much as possible, I try to cast whole casts, as opposed to just individuals in it. I also try to cast actors who are smart. Not necessarily book smart, but unafraid of using their noggin. It goes without saying (but I'll say it anyway) that I prefer actors who are instinctively generous on stage, both with their fellow actors and with the audience.

Being generous means that the actor in question puts the play and its story ahead of their part in it. It means being completely present on stage with their fellow performers, and receptive to listening and reacting to them. It means being open to the audience, and desirous of communicating to them, welcoming them into our collective story. A sense of humour is always an asset. Not being an asshole is preferable to the alternative.

Several years ago, I met the wonderful German director Wolfgang Kolnader, who has directed at various theatres around the world. He said to me that he thought Canadian stage actors were the best and most generous he had ever worked with. "Your system is probably the worst," he said. "You have no star system, no security for actors like we have in Europe where actors are part of a company for years, and you don't even get unemployment insurance. So instead of concentrating on their careers, your actors are there for the play. They give their all for the project and their fellow actors, instead of themselves." It made me both proud and sad. Couldn't we have both generosity and security? I wonder.

I tend to look for a really good actor who also seems to have an emotional connection with the material. I'd rather see an actor stretch to play a role than just be "playing themselves," whatever that means. And finally, the cast must reflect the diverse make-up of our society. Gender, different abilities, race, and many other factors always need addressing.

In professional sports, when teams are drafting future players, the choice becomes whether to pick a player who plays a specific position that your club needs, or to choose the best athlete, no matter the position they play. As well, the character of the young person is an important factor.

So, I tend to pick smart, flexible actors who are also good people… whenever possible.

It's an added bonus when a cast really gets along with each other; when their experience of working on a show lives on in their memory for a long time. It is, by definition, serendipity when that happens, but certainly casting does play a role in it (excuse the pun). Unfortunately, such chemistry is impossible to predict.

My feeling is that if I like the actors as people, and find them interesting, sympathetic and engaging, then there is a chance that they may like each other. The director is the common denominator. I've only ever run into problems when I haven't followed my instincts and the above guidelines.

Auditioning

Yuck. It's awful. I hate it. I try to avoid it whenever possible.

I will not audition anyone over forty, or if I've seen their work, or if I have worked with them before. I find there is only so much you can get from an audition, either from monologues or readings from the script. Some actors audition well and are not all that interesting. And others audition badly but are wonderful artists. I myself am a particularly bad auditionee.

I always read with the auditioning actor myself, preferring to experience what it's like to act with them. I find I can get a lot more information that way: about how present they are in the scene, what kind of listener they are, how potentially available to the input of their scene partner they might be, etc.

If you are someone who has the potential to grant employment, you are in a huge position of power. Put the auditionee at ease as much as you can. Be positive about their work. Don't cut them off in the middle of a monologue or when reading a scene. Don't lie to them, making it seem like you will let them know soon whether they will get the part when you have no intention of doing so. You don't have to lie to be kind.

Some directors try to put actors they are considering together for the audition to "test their chemistry." I find this absurd. Chemistry in a fifteen-minute audition? And what happens if they hate each other at first sight or are not a good fit? The audition for both individuals might hurt BOTH their chances.

Alternatively, they might get along famously when they first start, and if cast, grow to despise each other the more they get to know each other and work together. Or fake this chemistry in order to get the part.

"Chemistry" is not just about liking each other. More importantly, they should respect each other, and be open to working together and listening to what the other has to say, both on and off stage.

Casting Regrets

Don't have them.

You hired that actor for a reason. If they don't seem to be coming up with the goods, talk to them honestly and respectfully, offering help in a way that makes sense to them. You saw something that you felt was interesting for their portrayal. Remind them of what that was. If they're not rising to the challenge, it's probably your fault for not finding the right keys to help them.

In fact, I will always blame the director if I don't like a particular performance in a show I attend. If I feel the actor was miscast, that's the director's fault for choosing them. If I know the actor in question is a good actor and they're not good in this, that's the director's fault for not helping them properly or providing a strong enough context for their work.

I have never fired an actor for my mistake in casting them. I've only ever fired two actors, and both were because of how they behaved in rehearsal (one for being drunk on the job, another for abusive behaviour towards their colleagues) rather than the quality of their work *per se.*

As for the others, it was not their fault I cast them.

Working with Designers

We work in a stupid system, really. At least how it exists in most theatres across Canada.

A play is chosen. If it is a new work, it is sometimes workshopped. A director is chosen. They and/or the artistic director then choose designers for sets/props, costumes, lights, sometimes music, sometimes video, sometimes fights, choreography, intimacy, etc. At some point, the director and/or the artistic director casts the actors. And the meetings with individual designers begin.

The best description of a set design I ever heard was from designer Jim Plaxton, who said, "All sets are just acting machines." This to me exemplifies the purpose of design in the theatre. The designs of all components must feed and support the story and the storytellers. An image that is beautiful that lives in isolation from the narrative, no matter how breathtaking, is ultimately eye candy, and is as unsatisfying to the appetite as sweets are compared to nutritious food. Of course, we all want beautiful designs, but they must be directly relevant to the story being told and why we all are telling it.

Often, directors will work with various designers in isolation from the other designers. Set and costume designs usually need to be conceived and executed early on in the process. Other design elements, such as lights, sound, props and maybe video, are mostly created during rehearsals. But the physical world of the play will be discussed, drawn, reworked, and decided upon weeks — or even months — before rehearsals ever begin. More often than not, these designs are fixed and unable to be radically modified now that they are being built. We have learned to adapt to this stupid system because we have to, in much the same way that we have been forced to be able to mount different plays in exactly the same time frame as every other play: three-and-a-half weeks!

It has long been my fervent wish that we had a more flexible structure, where the first discussions between the director and the theatre would be about time and, by extension, money. Why are difficult and more experimental plays, new works, period pieces, and modern, perhaps more lightweight comedies all given exactly the same amount of time to rehearse? Can I trade part of the design budget for more time with the actors? Shouldn't theatre companies try to accommodate more complex pieces by providing them with more rehearsal time?

Therefore, we've become experts at "getting it up" in the time allotted. We often gear our total rehearsal schedule to relatively arbitrary yet quite rigid internal deadlines: "I better get the actors up on their feet by Day 5, in order to do a stumble-through on Day 12, in order to do a decent work-through and have another run (off book, hopefully) by the middle of Week 3, and then I get a few days to 'polish,' perhaps run once or twice more, before we move into the theatre and do tech work for two to three days, until we get back to the acting, by which time we have to be running with tech and have dress rehearsals and photo calls and media calls and previews and suddenly it's opening night and I'm done!"

Insane.

Sometimes designers on my productions who have been involved in the text work with actors, listening to the operative word exercise and its attendant discussions, have expressed to me that, had they had some of this input earlier, it might have enhanced or even changed their design concepts. Who could know what each actor brings to the whole? Who could guess what could be discovered collectively in rehearsal?

Sure, given the creativity and imagination of a director and designer, all kinds of interesting choices are often made. But wouldn't it be better if the performances and the staging and the design and every other element were all created at the same time, feeding off each other, adapting to influences and input from each other, and therefore be much more integrated with each other?

In the early '90s, I directed a new script for young audiences written by Dennis Foon entitled *Seesaw*. It dealt with changing status relationships, bullying, and self-image of children in their tweens. We wanted puppets to be used as the main theatrical image for the show. I was particularly interested in as many different kinds of puppetry as possible.

By the time we started on the project, all Dennis had was a basic idea, a thematic image, and some character sketches. Manitoba Theatre for Young People agreed to let us develop the work with a puppet designer from the very beginning. The brilliant Ronnie Burkett joined us, and we all started together.

We began by experimenting with lots of different kinds of puppets, which fed ideas to Dennis and me about the story and how it might be portrayed. Or sometimes Dennis would write a scene, and Ronnie would react to the content with ideas that took the material to unexpected levels of depth and complexity. I got to experiment with staging and production ideas in conjunction with these two brilliant collaborators. It was a truly joyful and fecund process.

It was really the only time in my career that the writing, the design, and the production all developed simultaneously. I wish I was able to work like that more often.

As I mentioned earlier, I will usually spend about a week on the text exercises; sometimes more, if I'm feeling especially fearless. It's wonderful when designers are there, and if they are, I get them to choose operative words from the point of view of their *métier*. Often, they will keep on going with the exercise on their own, even if they can't be in rehearsal doing it with us every day.

In my first conversations with designers before rehearsals, I'll often highlight words or phrases that speak to me strongly. These words usually deal with story and thematic ideas. I always start with content, not form. That is my preference. For me, content informs the image, not the other way around.

In order to discuss content, therefore, the text's strongest words or phrases are useful as a starting point, because once again, there are assumptions made about "issues" or "themes" that a given play may be addressing. It's one thing to say, "This play deals with the injustice of the oppressed," but another to say, "You know what jumps out at me? The phrase 'I feel hollow' in the context that it appears. What does that say to you?" Just like our text work with actors, this is a more specific, visceral and pragmatic discussion, and not an academic, intellectual exercise.

It is also essential to visit the performing space together with your set designer. Even if both of you know the space intimately, there is nothing like being in the actual location to spur the imagination. If you plan to reconfigure the performance area(s), try "acting" from those vantage points. Check sightlines, sound issues, lighting positions, backstage areas — all those factors that later might become problems. Sit everywhere in the audience and see if the experience of watching from different places changes the perspective of the experience.

When working with designers on the other elements — costumes, props, sound, video (if applicable) — it is important to make sure that all the elements live in the same theatrical world. Make sure that one element does not dominate any other, unless desired. Do they all add up to a coherent whole? Do they all create one world, no matter how stylized that world may be? Make sure the other designers understand their counterparts' work. At the first production meeting, which often happens before rehearsals begin, have each designer introduce their conceptual ideas and their work on realizing them, so that every designer understands every element.

The Politics of Collaboration

First, a few notes about the word "politics": from the Greek for citizen and city. Every play — indeed every human interaction — is inherently political. You cannot have any relationship in which status, position, or authority is not present in some way. This might include class or gender or age or education or race or sexual orientation or identification or any other factor which might need to be acknowledged in some way. In the same way, there are traditional hierarchies that need recognizing — and perhaps dismantling — in the theatre world. That they exist in the theatre and in the "real world" are inextricably linked. They are part and parcel of the sociopolitical framework that tends to govern all our interactions. Privilege and assumed authority have to be acknowledged, and those who have status need to listen and learn from those who have traditionally been denied access, equality and justice.

Secondly, politics and political thinking are emotional activities. People who call themselves "apolitical" often mistake political thought to be an intellectual pursuit, and therefore academic or self-indulgently theoretical. For me, how one looks at the world and its historical power imbalances creates a deeply primal reaction. Thought follows feeling, and how one responds to the political landscape is how one views humanity. My father would often say that the progressive is an optimist who believes that people will choose the greatest good for the greatest number over self-interest and greed, and that the reactionary is a cynic, only looking out for their own advancement, and that, these people believe, is the immutable nature of humanity.

Sometimes people's eyes glaze over at the mention of "political theatre." In the same way that Chekov is different from soap opera, good political theatre — good theatre, period — is specific. The way in to a political imperative is very often via the individual's struggle. It is through their eyes that the political message is illuminated. Brecht himself, that great political dramatist, said that the first duty of theatre is to entertain (remember that word?), because if the audience's attention is not held, they won't be listening to your political argument.

All of the above is meant to acknowledge the traditional power dynamics at play. Although the director may not be higher on the artistic evolutionary ladder than the designer, often designers have been taught that their job is to help the director realize their "vision." In fact, they become merely the facilitators of the director's ideas.

"Collaborate" comes from the Latin; *laborare* means "to work," "col" means "with"; *to work with.* Not to dictate or subjugate or bully or cajole or persuade or anything which amplifies an assumed power imbalance.

The first meeting(s) with designers are the most important, especially if you've never worked with them before. You want to be clear, with a developed sense of the content and aesthetic you have imagined, but yet leave lots of room for their input. Right from the beginning, set the tone of the collaborative nature of the relationship, but be honest if you feel that an idea is veering off the track.

That said, sometimes it is the director's job to be the conductor of the story. And human beings being human, not all relationships are smooth, respectful and completely collaborative.

The Exception That Proves the Rule

I was directing a play where we needed to transition from one reality to another. It needed to be relatively quick, as we were changing gears from a rather slow scene and needed an energy boost to take us to the next. I asked the lighting designer for a shortish transition of about three to five seconds between one state and the next. They refused, saying, "It'll look awful. It should be at least 25 seconds." They built it, we ran it, and it felt totally antithetical to the story we were telling. I tried persuading them, reasoning with them, and bargaining with them. Finally, I had to say, "I don't care how it looks. The story needs to move forward. You are in charge of the lights. I am in charge of telling the story. I know that this transition needs to be quick. If you want any input into how this transition looks, you had better make it happen now, otherwise it will be just be a straight cross fade in five seconds." Thankfully, they complied. Also, thankfully, in my career these irreconcilable power struggles have been extremely rare.

An Example of Mutual Problem Solving

I directed Rob Fothergill's fascinating play *Detaining Mr. Trotsky* at the Toronto Free Theatre in the late '80s. The late and immensely talented John Ferguson designed a rat's maze of a set, with the walls of the labyrinth covered with chicken wire. Most of the play was set in a POW camp in Amherst, Nova Scotia in 1917, and this image worked effectively on many different levels. After about two weeks of working in the rehearsal hall with tape on the floor indicating where these barriers were, I was finding the main acting area somewhat too confined, especially in terms of its depth. I asked John to help me solve this problem. We hit on the idea of moving the furthest upstage barrier, which created an effective crossover used in our scene transitions, to the back wall, adding three more feet of depth downstage, but losing the most upstage corridor. John argued it wasn't as effective a design. I totally agreed, but argued the actors needed space to tell the story much more than they needed to act on a beautiful set. John finally agreed, and was able to make it work in an artistically satisfying way. In my opening night card, he simply wrote, "Dearest Richard. You were right. Love John."

The collaborative nature of the relationship between a designer and a director is, I believe, exactly the same relationship with the actor, or the playwright, or anyone else involved in the production. The best collaborations are when both parties are excited by each other's contributions, and the shared vision grows from each, adding idea upon idea, which becomes something way more interesting than either could have reached separately. When that happens, neither can remember whose idea was whose. And neither cares.

7

Rehearsal

What Is Rehearsal?

Not as silly a question as it seems.

Back to the etymology: "to harrow again," as in cultivating soil…
again. It also means to tell again or repeat (the French word for
rehearsal is *répétition*). So, in whatever meaning, the concept of
going over again and again seems constant. But how to go over
again and again?

In my experience, there are two negative types of roles that directors
assume that are both mistakes for them to adopt: the Non-Director
and the Over-Director. For whatever reason, directors sometimes
slip into these roles, almost without realizing that they are doing
so.

o o o

The Non-Director is more common. The Non-Director
skims over the surface, again and again and again, never

getting anywhere close to the depth the piece might deserve. I performed in a Shakespeare play where the director said on the first day of rehearsals, "This play is an iceberg; one tenth above the surface, and nine tenths below. Our job is to do the one tenth and let the nine tenths speak for itself." It was a very shallow production.

o o o

I truly believe they don't know how to work, or more accurately, how to rehearse. They watch the actors flail their way through the scenes, offering little or no real help. What notes they do give have very little context as to what is trying to be achieved, which probably wasn't discussed in the first place. Scenes are run, never worked on in any meaningful detail. The scenes are not broken down into smaller sections and/or moments of action. Very soon into the process, these directors want to see run-throughs of the whole play, saying, "I can't really tell what is missing or what is too much until I see the whole thing."

So, you run — often — and very little changes between each run because nothing is subsequently worked on. Actors are left to explore on their own, and so there is little sense of unity of purpose or intention amongst the whole group. Bit by bit, most good actors tend to figure things out for themselves, but in this situation, everyone is working in a vacuum, within their own bubble of individualized invention. Sometimes Non-Directors are saved by their casts. The actors may even do communal work in secret, desperately trying to fill the void left by their Non-Director. Their desperation can create a kind of raw energy that can be quite watchable, and even some strong moments, but ultimately, chances are there is little substantive cohesion in the production.

o o o

The Over-Director is just as bad, if not worse. The Over-Director delves into minutiae, sometimes endlessly rehearsing the beginning of the play, or some other section, and rarely getting to the other scenes. I once performed in a Shakespeare piece where the first time we ever did the very last scene was on the first preview performance. It was not a strong ending to the play.

O O O

The Over-Director is usually so insecure as to be afraid of their actors actually speaking up or disagreeing with their direction. They will often say the first thing that comes into their head, without considering the implications those words may have. They may be abrasive or rude. They tend to be result-oriented, and don't take the time to understand the individual processes each actor needs to produce their best work. Their philosophy often consists of "divide and conquer" and they can be afraid of the natural camaraderie that will usually develop amongst a cast which, by definition, must exclude the director.

In bad rehearsal situations, this fellowship is often the only saving grace in a miserable working environment, and the Over-Director will become more and more isolated and lose more and more respect, often without even knowing, because they refuse to acknowledge the actors' artistic integrity and the invaluable contributions they can bring to the overall production. Any respect that is shown to these directors is born from their position of power only, which they will probably mistake for genuine deference.

Clearly, these are archetypes. Rarely does one person totally inhabit all of these traits of either kind of these directors. They may even exhibit parts of each simultaneously. And sometimes, even good directors can take on one or more of the characteristics of one. It is a constant struggle to maintain good and healthy creative processes, especially in the face of time or money constraints, difficult personalities or unsympathetic producers. But struggle we must.

O O O

There is, of course, another heinous kind: the Abusive Director. All too slowly, but bit by bit, I fervently believe this dinosaur is becoming extinct, thanks to some brave individuals — the vast majority being women — who bring their abuse to light. The mistreatment may or may not include gender-based insults, actual sexual assault, or belittling remarks. Needless to say, under no circumstances is this behaviour ever remotely acceptable, and it must be called out whenever witnessed. It is bullying, plain and simple.

O O O

For far too long, the director has held an exalted, unearned position of authority, based on some power hierarchy long obsolete, and/or sometimes in the name of "artistic vision." In the same way we have witnessed men in authority using their privilege to assault the vulnerable, so too have I witnessed similar abuses by directors or artistic directors, both men and women, who feel that they can say or act as they wish simply because they have the power to grant or deny employment.

There is nothing inherent in the job description of being a director which allows for such behaviour. NOTHING! The past excuses of mistreatment to get at "real" emotions or being "passionate" to challenge the actor to show more are total bullshit. It's like an abusive person hitting their partner "out of love." It is a contradiction in terms, and besides being unethical, is also counter-productive to good and *truly* passionate work. Those come from a feeling of safety and trust, not fear and intimidation.

The director is not "above" the other artists in a production. Their job is "outside," as it encompasses an objective eye and ear, and often, but not always, initiates the creation of the world of the production. But that doesn't imply a status more elevated than anyone else's. This is not just about equity or morality. Respectful, egalitarian processes create better art.

Values

To that end, the times are a-changin', even in the tradition-laden world of the theatre.

> I recently directed an opera called *Hook Up*, written by Julie Tepperman (librettist) and Chris Thornborrow (composer). The piece dealt with sexual consent and assault at a Canadian university. The material was powerful; both emotional and evocative. There was the potential for difficult and vulnerable episodes for the actors, especially for the lead character who is assaulted in the story.
>
> On the first day, one of the performers suggested that we all anonymously write down a value we would like to see practised during rehearsals, and then have them read out by the stage manager. People wrote about respect, sensitivity, empathy, kindness, and patience. There was also a request for some lightness at the end of each day: a communal song, or joke, or just a check-in about how everyone was doing.
>
> This is an example of the new normal where actors are empowering themselves to look after each other. As the director, I found it moving and humbling, and was extremely proud of this group's strength and commitment to each other and the material.

This new generation of theatre artists are working to right traditional wrongs or unaddressed issues that have never really been dealt with. The new requirement for hiring intimacy coaches is a strong innovation. Becoming more aware of off-colour jokes, or unasked-for physicality, or even asking by what pronouns people are called are all positive advances.

This is not "political correctness." This is the death throes of a straight-white-male-dominated culture, and as one of those, I for one am happy to see this culture disappear.

First Steps after Text Work

You've done your text work! You get the actors up from the table! The actors are champing at the bit. They are like thoroughbred race horses, ready to gallop towards the finish line. But they aren't nearly ready to even canter yet. They can barely walk.

I take the first go-through on one's feet slowly, painstakingly. Too often, this phase is purely slapdash, surface exploration, with actors trying anything and everything, while the director "lets them play" (see Non-Director above). Not much is learned by that at this point, I feel. It's looseness for its own sake, instead of an exploratory exercise with a considered agenda. I believe in working in great detail, but without setting anything in stone. Try things a number of ways, but there's no need to say, "This is the right one!" Yet. There ARE times when one needs to shut up and let the actors go for a bit, but first, everything needs to be addressed. At least we should begin to know what we don't know. You may remind the actors of their operative words, and what was learned from the text exercises. Be clear as to what we all might be going for in a given scene or given moment, and perhaps what we don't know yet. Always try to keep the goals in sight, rather than exploration without purpose.

Conversely, some directors start to intricately stage everything right away, and expect it to be repeated every time in exactly the way it was first staged (see Over-Director above). There's no exploration, no actor input. Perhaps the director has worked it all out at home or is good at making it up on the spot and wants to "give a structure" in order for the actor to start to explore. It seldom works that way, of course, because then the actors are committed to repeating work that has been set and are just trying to reproduce the director's choices and try to make those constraints work. The actors become as life-like as the little models the director may have used in the mock-up of the set provided by the set designer.

I also start to stage transitions in this first work-through. Some directors just jump over them in the first or even second pass of their work, leaving them to do later, like an unpleasant chore that is put off until the last possible moment. But transitions are an essential component of the staging, and the movement and pace of them are just as important as scene work.

Don't coast. Explore. Don't skim. Dig. Ask questions. Offer options. Engage everything.

Again, it is the actor who is the ultimate storyteller. If they are unclear or uncomfortable, chances are the most interesting and provocative work will not be allowed to emerge until those issues are addressed. So, address them. Encourage the actor to just try their idea, instead of talking about it. Better to have many options, rather than one set during the first pass-through.

Now, of course, every play is different, and to prescribe the same methodology to different texts is ridiculous. Except for a few consistencies (such as the text work laid out in Part 1), the process of how one rehearses may be as varied as the material. Different scripts demand different priorities, and therefore different processes. But as you gain more experience, you will find certain consistent ways of working that work best for you and your collaborators. Similarly, there might be time constraints that demand different approaches. Actors are just as aware of the time there is to work as is the director. Discuss your approach with them and get their input if they have concerns.

"Blocking"...

... should be declared an obsolete term. Words are important, and if one calls something by a name, some sense of that word will seep into the very fabric of the activity. Everything about the term "blocking" seems antithetical to artistic exploration. The term is meant, I think, as in "to set," as in blocking something (a hat, a piece of wood?) that excludes other possibilities so that the "right" choices are fixed and immutable.

No matter how the term came into common theatrical usage, it is totally anachronistic. Staging is an expression of the story. In some cases, it can be quite fluid, changing nightly in performance, depending on the circumstances. In some productions, it might be highly stylized and choreographed, and set to music so as to be exact and consistent. Mostly — ideally — pieces become relatively set in their movement because that staging illuminates the story and the dramatic or comic imperatives, but other factors, such as lights, video, or sightlines obviously play their parts in its formation. In most cases, the staging of a play needs the same collaboration and dialogue between director and actor that the exploration of the text demanded earlier in the process.

I would never presume to prescribe anything about staging, or any other ideas to do with interpretation, to another director. These are choices that are clearly personal and individual, and specific to the artist and their collaborators. What matters is *how* one communicates to one's collaborators, and if the choices are tied to an intention that is playable for the actor.

What I have learned over the years is that the main process of making artistic choices is to identify what you, the artist, likes and responds most strongly to, both as an audience member and as a practitioner.

It is a lifetime's work to discover and hone one's own taste, and to figure out what specifically inspires you and fuels your imagination. It is another lifetime's work figuring out how to communicate these choices, and yet another lifetime to realize them. By my calculations, that's three lifetimes. This work is endlessly difficult, and the chances of real success — judged by one's own exacting standards and not by others' — are rare.

I mostly prefer relatively rigorous staging, where every move has been considered and chosen. I try to make sure that within this structure, there is room for spontaneity and growth — not for its own sake, but as a genuine maturation. The actor who "changes it up" just because they're bored or because their attention span has found its end point, is often swimming in self-indulgent waters. If, by listening and gradual evolution between scene partners, the feel of the scene transforms, perhaps to the point where the staging has altered, then this is most likely a natural continuation of the work. However, there might be all kinds of instances where this is not desired. such as if lighting is affected, or if this new direction is counter to the agreed spirit of the content.

Staging…

… should not be created at home with little figures on the set model or ground plan.

The most I ever have in my head before rehearsals begin are some images, and those are never hard and fast. They come via the text, and sometimes they're worth following through, and other times not so much. They might be a picture, or a movement pattern, or distances between characters, or even from where characters enter or exit on the stage. But it's impossible for me to essentially pre-plan the staging without real bodies in real space and time, not to mention the actor's input. These images will most likely change and evolve when working in a space with those real people, with their real hearts and real brains.

In the late '80s I worked with the great actress Patricia Hamilton in *The Trial of Judith K.*, Sally Clark's adaptation of Kafka's *The Trial*, and we were just beginning to stage. I started giving Patsy all kinds of business, including props usage and intricate moves around the stage, until she stopped me, saying, "I like these ideas, but I always find that I can take more ownership of my moves when it's from my initiation that I can try out first. Then if there's something missing or going in a wrong direction, give me your ideas."

Another wonderful actor, Tom MacBeath, once told me early on in a rehearsal process, "I respond best to general directions at first. Give me large brush strokes to begin with, and as the process continues, we can get to the finer points."

I love it when actors tell me how they work and what direction works best for them.

Actors need to know why they are being asked to move where they are being asked to move. Movement reveals story, character, thematic imagery, and/or moments of beauty. But that movement must be inextricably linked to the text and context of the story.

Many ideas will certainly flow based on the detailed text work we've already done. What's happening between characters, and where we are in terms of the emotional journey of both the characters and the story, might automatically suggest some movement. For instance, if we have discussed that a character is reaching out to another, and that person is avoiding that connection, some obvious movement patterns might appear to be in play. Those choices might be too obvious, however, and might want to be worked against, but at least this movement emanates from the communal work already done and is a starting point for exploration. Images can often be useful at the beginning, such as, "This is a bit of an interrogation, isn't it?" or "Is this a dance of some kind?," etc. The nature of the physical parameters (the set design) will obviously determine much as well, but within those confines there might be infinite possibilities.

As well, there might be an aesthetic that wants to be explored: stillness, abstract movement patterns, non-naturalistic images, etc. These should be inspired, as always, from the content of the story. Both the interpreters (the actors) and the witnesses (the audience) should feel that somehow the movement, however stylized, emanates from a sense of why the choice was made, and not just because the director thought it would be different, or cool, or beautiful, or anything other than the sense and intentions of the storytelling.

Problems need to be seen as opportunities, and challenges should always be approached as potential for creativity. Try lots of stuff — specifically explained — in different ways. Encourage the actors to initiate, but not in a vacuum. You can provide context (intention, action, or subtext), so that their exploration will be tied to the specific, rather than just exploration for its own sake. Whenever an actor says, "Can I try this?" I always tell them that they don't need to ask, they should just do it. Directors should offer options rather than limits, unless those limits might possibly be liberating.

> Miles Potter directed me in *For the Pleasure of Seeing Her Again* by Michel Tremblay and suggested that my character should stay in physical contact with a kitchen chair for the entire play until the very last scene. The scenes were separated by decades in the story, so how a small child sat in the chair, as opposed to a teenager, or a young adult, or a middle-aged man, offered me surprisingly limitless possibilities and creative opportunities. It was entirely liberating to be so confined. It was an example of how a directorial image became a freeing direction.

All of this is, of course, variable depending on the actor one is directing. Some love a basic staging structure right away, and find it freeing. Others like to "wing it." I don't mind adjusting either way, as long as it's clear what is ultimately at the heart of the content, and therefore how that might translate as staging. Again, too much structure might be limiting, too little might be self-indulgent and ill-defined. The balance is all.

The Next Work-Throughs

I often think of a rehearsal process as divided into several work-throughs. I feel lucky if I am able to get through three complete go-throughs before moving into technical rehearsals. After the table work, the first slow work-through might take a week or so to complete, followed by a stumble-through (my friend and colleague Jani Lauzon calls them "humble-throughs") of the whole piece. This is not just for the actors' benefit. Set, costume, lighting, video (if applicable) and sound designers may all need to see how the show is progressing and how it will affect their contribution.

The second work-through might be a good deadline to try and get the actors off book. We are now probably over halfway through our total time. Without panic, it might be good to remind everyone that the time is finite. This work-through is combining several agenda items concurrently. It's still about investigation, but certain options may feel "right," and act as signposts for further choices. These choices might include decisions about character, relationships, staging, builds of tension and/or conflict, pacing, or anything else that seems to leap up and say, "this makes sense."

I usually start each scene in the second work-through with a line run off book, then begin to work the scene in detail, and finish by running that scene. I also make sure to include transitions in this scene run — both the ones before and after the scene — if applicable. It's important to get these moments in the actors' and stage manger's bodies (assuming they are doing the transitions and not stage crew) as soon as you start to run scenes. Again, it means that they are integral parts of the whole.

It might take almost as much time doing this work-through as the first, since certain other factors, such as being off book, and going into greater detail, are being added. Once we've finished this second work-through, it's vital to have another run of the whole piece. Most certainly the designers will need to see it again, as well as any other crew or staff, including the artistic director or producer, who need to see how the production is taking shape.

The third work-through might be even more constrained by time. You might have only three days or so to work through the whole piece. Unless it is needed, I might dispense with the line run before each scene, although a complete line run might be useful at some point (see later in this chapter re: line runs).

This third work-through is more about honing, perhaps editing moments, and looking at the longer lines of action. When we started our text work, we were looking at every word, every stage direction, punctuation, and the smallest details. Our first work-through on our feet was examining moments of action, phrases of dialogue. The second work-through was concentrating more about each scene as a unit. This third work-through can explore longer sections. As you work through, you might run larger chunks than just a scene. Maybe divided into the five parts of the narrative structure? Or whatever division makes sense to you.

Then finish with another run-through of the whole piece. Always leave enough time for notes after any and all run-throughs, whether of a scene or a larger section or the whole play. Actors crave specific feedback, and notes can also set an agenda as to what needs further work in rehearsal. Much more on that later.

Be Creative

If a scene happens in a hallway, find a hallway to rehearse for a bit. Or if the scene takes place on either side of a door, or outside, or any other location you can easily find or recreate, try it there to get at some verisimilitude.

If the dialogue is interrupted by another character interjecting in another theatrical reality, such as a ghost figure (like Isobel in *Lion in the Streets*), rehearse the scene without the interjections. If a character is talking to someone whom we don't see or hear, get someone to play that person, with possible answers. Or better yet, play it yourself.

> I directed Noah Reid in *Sudden Death*, Charlotte Corbeil-Coleman's play at the National Theatre School. There was a particularly heartbreaking scene where Noah's character, who was based on the hockey player John Kordic, is talking to his father through a closed door. John is desperately seeking his father's approval, and the father refuses to give it. We don't hear the father's dialogue, and he is not a character who ever appears on stage, but he's a monumental figure in John's life.

It was hard for Noah to access this scene. He was playing to a door. He needed to get a specific feeling as to who that figure was on the other side: how he talked, how much he spoke, and exactly how he dismissed and hurt his son. I played the dad, on the other side of the door, not saying much, but just enough for Noah to feel his father's disappointment in him, and the scene came alive for him with a specificity and nuance he couldn't possibly manufacture on his own.

If a character has a monologue, it first needs to be decided to whom it is being said. Then you can provide them an "audience." For instance, if it's an inner monologue, get the actor to play it to themselves in a mirror. Or get them to record it and play it back so they can just listen to their internal voice. If it is to the audience, get the actor to play it to one person, very close, just enough for the other person to hear, to create intimacy. Then get them to talk to everyone in the room, making eye contact, to communicate individually and specifically. These techniques hold even more importance in directing a solo show, of course. In a sense, the audience needs to be "cast" as a character.

If there is an intimate, private scene, I often ask the actors to sit very close together to talk quietly between themselves, making sure nobody else can hear them. Much of acting is about the dynamic between the private and the public: what we say and what we don't, what we choose to reveal and when and to whom, what is the "truth" and what is cover-up, etc. Create some privacy before opening it up to be viewed by all.

In "real life," we would die of embarrassment if certain scenes of intimacy were viewed by others. And yet, actors love to explore these intimate moments in order to access an emotional wellspring before an audience. It is this conflict between the public and the private that is the tension and emotional underpinning of the action. It is the essence of subtext.

Life doesn't happen on a stage. Plays do. Life happens where the plays are set. Get away from stage life, and insert real life, to broaden the scope and to be more rigorously specific.

Improvisation

Some actors hate it, others love it. I believe that mostly the actors that hate it either haven't done it enough or have misconceptions about what it is and how it can be useful.

When using this technique in a text-based work, be specific about why the actors are being asked to improvise. What is the aim of the exercise? What qualities are we trying to get at? Of course, the point of improvising is to not go for results, but to let the improv take you where it leads, or at least where the collective impulses lead. But the actors should know why time is spent on this instead of "rehearsing."

These improvisations are NOT about creating material (text), but about filling in the richness behind or underneath or surrounding the existing material (context). It might be a scene that is talked about but is not in the play. It might be a scene from their backstory. It might be an imagined encounter between characters, or when and how they first met. It might be one character's fantasy about how the other character should behave. It might an out-of-reality situation, such as the famous "hot seat exercise," where one character must defend themselves from an interrogation from the other characters.

I have sometimes had other actors read the text of a different character, asking them to avoid giving too much expression, and get the actor playing that character to stand beside "themselves" and speak their subtext. Sometimes I have asked the actor to distill their overall desire of what they want/need from their scene partner, and put it in the form of a command, such as "Listen to me!" or "Love me!" or "Shut up!" and allow them to say that imperative at three points within the scene.

Use your imagination. But use your discretion. Like everything else, this tool must be used sparingly, or it will become blunt from overuse and not achieve the desired result, which is to find the specificity and richness to enhance the text. Besides, you actually do need to rehearse the play!

Getting at the "Stuff"

The real point of rehearsal.

Again, it is almost always best to ask questions rather than tell actors what something means. "What's going on at this moment?" is always a useful question. Questions could be about subtext ("What does she really mean when she says this?"), intention ("Why is he doing this now, and not later?"), or even staging ("Do they want to get away here or move in?"). Now, sometimes it might be easier to just say, "Why don't you try moving in there." instead of putting it as a question, but even this is just a suggestion — an offer — and not a directive.

The "stuff" in question is about the emotional range of the characters in the story. How do we mine it? How do we access the pain or turmoil or joy or any other emotional heights or depths the story demands? But to follow through on the metaphor, raw materials that are mined need refining, or otherwise they might become self-indulgent.

My late son Luke was a great fan of *The Lord of the Rings* books and films, as am I. When the last film of the trilogy, *The Return of the King*, was released, we were among the first to stand in line to see it. We watched the film in great anticipation, and after it was over, I asked him how he liked it. "I was a bit disappointed," he said. "I was expecting to be more moved than I was." I agreed with him, and asked why he thought that was the case. He replied, "I think *they* were crying so much, there was no room for *me* to cry."

Often, because time is limited and we mostly tend to be result-oriented, we accept the first viable pass that makes sense and want it set for the life of the production. There might be other options. There might be more depth, something more interesting, less obvious. It might be faster, or slower, or simpler. Or maybe there's other interpretations of the same text.

The point is to respect the fact that the art form is essentially process-oriented, and not try to push for "results" immediately. Besides, what is the end result of a piece of theatre? Is it the opening night? The best night of the run? The closing? The middle of an extended run of a transfer to Broadway? Does it even exist? The most you can do as a director is to provide the *context* for the performers to continue working towards the common goal of telling the story as interestingly, engagingly, and provocatively as possible, each and every time it is performed.

And sometimes, there are surprises in the interpretation.

Way back in the late '70s, I was directing a workshop of Neil Munro's play *ECU*. It was about a terminally ill older actor on a film set for a public service announcement about drinking and driving. With him were his assistant and a young university student reporter. The play was littered with film references and jokes.

At the climax of the play, the actor collapses in a semi-comatose state. The assistant takes out two vials of medicine to inject into him. As he does, he recites the classic Danny Kaye routine from *The Court Jester* — "The pellet with the poison's in the vessel with the pestle, the chalice from the palace has the brew that is true." I got up from the table and talked to the actor playing the assistant, explaining he had two choices: he could euthanize his boss with "the pellet with the poison," which might be a kind, humane act, or save him with "the brew that is true." It gave the bit a huge resonance, and the action was rich with emotional subtext.

As I sat down again, Neil whispered in my ear, "I never meant that. I was just writing some schtick. But I like it." Sometimes, even playwrights don't know what depths are contained in their words.

Spacing and Rhythm

These are two aspects of directing that are sometimes misunderstood, over-emphasized, or completely underestimated, and should not be confused with staging and pacing.

I define spacing as somewhat different than staging *per se* and is something I look at as the staging becomes solidified in the later stages of rehearsal. It is the amount of space *between* characters, or how multiple actors are placed in space, and again, must reflect content, however that may be interpreted.

So, what is in this space between characters? Electricity, tension, mistrust, love...it can be any one of a million things. But it is the space between them that defines where they are, and not where they are that defines the space between them. There always has to be something in that space. How that space changes: expands or contracts, becomes fluid or rigid, and attracts or repels each of the characters is, in many ways, the major determining factor for its staging. We may think it's about moving bodies in space, but in fact, it's more about exploring the space between those bodies that informs the movement. When an actor is alone on stage, the other body is the audience. But then again, the audience is always another part in the equation, and the space between it and each performer is always a major determining factor.

Similarly, rhythm is determined by silence and stillness even more than by speed of speech or of action. The old adage is that speed is the rate of speaking, while pace is the tightness of cues being picked up between the actors. But for me, what defines pace is not necessarily just the tightness of the cues, but by when and how the dialogue is punctuated with a beat or pause. Like the words in our operative word exercises, overuse of any one thing or word starts to devalue that thing. Too many pauses become ineffective, predictable, and enervating. Too much pace becomes meaningless or turns into pace for its own sake without substance.

The script might require — or you as the director might prefer — a breakneck speed, but the actors need to build to that pace. If you have the pace without a full investigation of the full scope of what is there, then the fast pace will be hollow and without basis. In order for the subtext to be rich and complex, you need to thoroughly examine it, and only then hide it from view, *under* the text. Otherwise it will be truly non-existent.

Now, I must confess to a bias towards fast-moving dialogue. I like thinking with the actors, or even slightly behind them, so that I have to stay alert to the speed of their thoughts. You don't want the audience thinking faster than the actors and anticipating what's coming next. But you also don't want the audience to get lost in a fast pace and lose nuance, subtlety, or complexity.

Silence and stillness can be breathtaking. For me, the contrast is all. Like music, there is a heartbeat to pace; a rhythm, which rises and falls, surprises and evolves, grows and wanes.

The pace should keep an audience awake and alert, ready to listen and react with the actors.

Sometimes actors will start to talk quicker when asked to "pick up the pace." Pace is usually associated with the speed at which the cues between actors is contracted so that there is less space between them. But pace does not necessarily mean fast. Finding the rhythm of a particular piece, or for that matter, even a particular section of a scene, is found more by listening rather than imposing. Usually actors have to work up to a particular pace, whatever it may be. "Well paced" is almost always meant as synonymous with quick. But it isn't.

I directed a production of Jason Sherman's *The League of Nathans* in Winnipeg in the '90s. Michael Healey and Jordan Pettle played two of the Nathans, ex-best friends who meet after many years, each thinking the other has set up the meeting. They see each other, and the text just says, "Long pause." They asked me how long the pause should last. I said, "Let's see." Over the course of the run, the pause grew to over 90 seconds. During it, neither moved nor made any sound. It went past the audience's discomfort, past their worry that they had forgotten their lines, past their confusion, past their potential annoyance, and approached the limits of their patience. All of these were entirely appropriate for these two characters in this situation.

The Devil in the Details

An addendum of specificity. And a warning.

Detail can be a rabbit hole. One can go down it and lose sight of the larger issues, and meanwhile, the audience may not even notice some of this attention to detail.

O O O

Alfred Hitchcock, the great film director, used to say that he was not responsible for "fridge moments." When asked what those were, he answered (and I'm paraphrasing), "I'm only responsible for the audience while they are in the theatre. When they go home, go to bed, and wake up in the middle of the night to go to the kitchen for a bite or a drink, open the fridge, and while they are getting their snack, suddenly stop and think, "Wait a minute. That doesn't make sense!" about something they saw in my film, I'm not responsible for that."

O O O

Producing art is an obsessive enterprise. We artists are often consumed with the minutiae of creation. We will worry a small thing to death, trying to wrestle it the ground and bend it to our conceptual will. Or we fall in love with a moment, or an idea, or a *soupçon* of a detail which seems to make our hearts sing. This can be a strong element of one's production, or it might be a distraction from what is truly important: the story.

The trick is discerning which is which. We must be willing to let go of our most precious ideas if they do not serve the whole (writers sometimes horrifically call this "killing your babies"). And we must not let one moment overtake the larger priorities that need attention. Get to know your own foibles. And be ruthless with your creative offspring. They are simply ideas, and if they don't belong in the big picture, have the courage to cut them loose.

Runs vs. Work

I don't believe in running the whole play often. I consider runs precious. They have much to teach, but must be used sparingly, or their worth will diminish from overuse, like a word that is repeated over and over until its power is gone. As well, mistakes tend to become entrenched from too many runs, and smaller sections that might need reworking, re-conceiving, tweaking or just more attempts, are untended. Work smaller sections and run those if need be but save your complete run-throughs for when they are most useful, like after completing a full work-through.

For me, the most exciting part of rehearsing is the conversation and exploration between the actors and the director. There can sometimes be some tension there. That can be a good thing, if it's a respectful disagreement and based purely on the work. The danger can be that there is too much talking and not enough doing. If the actor has an idea or wants to try something, the best thing for them to do is just to try it, without talking too much about it. After making several attempts at different approaches, the conversation will then have a context (there's that word again!) for a decent dialogue. It will be a much shorter discussion than one that is purely theoretical, and there is a shared vocabulary for the discussion.

As time begins to diminish towards the end of the rehearsal period, I will also solicit input from the actors about what needs working on (I call it "Actors' Choice"). Only the actor can tell you what their needs and areas of confusion or insecurities are. As valuable as your outside eye and ear are, so too is the inside experience of the performer. If the actor is unsure about a section or scene or moment or even a word, they have to feel safe and free to communicate that to you so it can be addressed. Similarly, your position as the outside eye is vital to identify what sections need more work from an "objective" point of view.

When I first started directing, I would sometimes get frustrated by actors asking so many questions or seeming to need lots of information from me. "Get on with it!" my inner self was screaming. There's too much to do without all this need for talking or exploring countless options. I think this feeling comes from a sense of fear, that you the director will be revealed as having no business being in charge of the whole production. It is this same fear that fuels the irrational instinct that the director must have all the answers all the time. A director's insecurity is as powerful and can be as pervasive and debilitating as any actor's is.

Line Runs

An underrated activity.

The priority is to try to get the page out of the actors' brains. Most of us memorize by taking a photograph of the written script. You can almost see the actor turning the page in their head. You very often can tell when an actor is coming up to a large speech. You see them prepare for this large chunk of text that they're about to tackle.

I believe in being exact with the text. After all the careful work to decipher every single clue, including stage directions, punctuation, grammatical oddities and the etymology of words, not to be exact would be counter to our work. It usually falls to the stage manager or their assistant to give line notes to actors. As an actor, I prefer mine in writing, so that I can study my mistakes before the next run-through or the next time we work the scene in which I made my mistakes.

As a director, I encourage this attention to accuracy. I make sure that the cast understands that I have authorized the stage manager to keep giving line notes for the length of the run, if need be. If it's a new play, getting a line of dialogue even slightly wrong is disrespectful to the playwright. Of course, the actor can request a change and, if it is approved by the writer and director, go ahead and change it.

The aim is to try as much as possible to remove the page from the actor's inner eye and move the words to their mouth. The movement and speech of the scene can then be lived in the moment on the stage, and not on the page in the actor's head. Repeated line runs can help in facilitating this muscle memory so that the lines feel immediate rather than recalled. If this is achieved, the actor can then concentrate on being present, instead of thinking about what they're supposed to say next after their scene partner/s have finished talking. Make sure the actors understand that this is not simply a technical exercise to memorize the text that lives outside of the process, but an integral part of rehearsals: to encourage listening, to install a sense of play, and to engage the cast to react, both to their scene partners and to the play as a whole.

If the director is present at the line run, some suggestions or notes can be given and a scene or part of a scene can be repeated with the change(s). Even a line run can be used as a work opportunity.

Often, it is possible to add elements to this essentially pragmatic exercise to gain some insight away from the staging elements. Fast pacing is useful to quicken the speed of thought but retaining the intention of the moment. Whispering can heighten the urgency of communication. Getting the actors to the extreme edges of the rehearsal space so that they need to talk loudly can do something similar. Or sitting in a tight circle with constant eye contact. More enhanced listening is always the main goal.

By changing certain factors for the line run, different impulses may provide some new information that might add to the resonance of the scene. And the added task of thinking about something else while running lines can be totally helpful in the memorization of the text.

Sometimes I will do a "movement" line run, in which nothing is spoken. The actors do their movement in the space and follow the course they take when doing the whole text. It is important that the actors not mouth the words or otherwise play the text, but rather concentrate on the patterns and paths they take around the stage and see if that illuminates anything about the story or the interactions between the characters. Eliminating factors can be as informative as adding them.

I have also done line runs where the actors move wherever they wish throughout the space while speaking and listening to the text: joining groups, creating contact, breaking contact, listening and observing, or anything else that might occur. The only rule is that they must be in constant motion, never stationary or sedentary, even if they aren't in a given scene. They should not follow the movement patterns that have been staged. It is a movement improvisation utilizing the written dialogue. See what happens. There might even be a staging idea that is revealed and might be useful to incorporate.

8

Scheduling

There is never enough time. Ever. I would love to spend a day on tasks for which I can only afford an hour. A week to focus on things that only get a day. And a month to work on things when I only have a week. So, time management is vital.

In Canada, we have traditionally rehearsed six days a week, eight hours a day (they do give us an hour for lunch and five minutes of breaks for every hour worked!) Madness. In a rep situation, the total time span is usually greater, but most often the hours add up to approximately the same. Of course, you can always form a company, and you can work how and when you want over a protracted period of time. Lots of artistic freedom and flexibility, but how to finance this increased period of time might be an issue. And usually the artists have to find this money themselves. That said, there are ongoing negotiations within the Canadian theatre community to create more flexible models. Again, money is always a major issue, especially in the not-for-profit sector where government subsidy is always precarious, and private fundraising is under pressure due to increased competition, never mind a pandemic.

Good rehearsals are exhausting. Creative endeavours are, more often than not, emotionally draining. I find that after five or six hours of work, the law of diminishing returns comes into play. Working six days a week, with only one day off to do chores AND learn your lines or even just think about the text, can be counterproductive. Not to mention inhuman. A personal life is not only good for one's mental health, it's also an important part of one's work. It keeps you grounded, it puts things in perspective, and it connects you to a well of emotional availability, if you let it. And every artist needs time and space away from the intensity of the work to allow their brains to recharge and make room for ideas without the immediate pressure to produce. Some of my best ideas have come while I'm doing the dishes.

In Britain, they generally work five-and-a-half days per week. The last day of the work week is only a four-hour call. Not a bad system. However, I think it's high time the theatre joined the vast majority of the working world and work five days a week for rehearsals, even if you have to change to a six-day week during the run. I also like to work six hours in a seven-hour span, in two blocks of three hours each, separated by an hour for lunch, and with a fifteen-minute break in the middle of each block. Working shorter hours more intensely, rather than longer and less vigorously, works best for me. This is not always possible, but it is my preferred schedule.

It is important that you find your own optimum rhythm for your best work. You will have to adapt your schedule due to certain external factors (this actor has an ongoing voice gig that they can't give up, this other actor has childcare issues, etc.), but it is good for you to know the best choice for you. And always be aware of how long your actors can work effectively. That said, I am fascinated to try working with new, more flexible models to rethink the accepted norms of workplace structures.

The Big Picture

So, you've got a finite amount of time. Maybe you've spent a week doing text work. Much is known, but nothing is set. You now have two-and-a-half weeks, on average, to stage the show, rehearse, make changes to the staging, make sure the actors are confidently off book, help them understand their characters and the story as a whole, be open to discover unlooked-for moments, go deeper, and then go deeper still, make sure the pace is strong, etc., etc., etc. And all of this before the technical elements are added. And all of that is not accounting for a new play, with its possible multiple rewrites.

As the director, you need to pace the rehearsal period as much as you need to pace the show. And you also have to know how to rehearse.

Each show has its own pace, in both its execution and in its rehearsal rhythm. What might take a two-hour call to work on can take a day on another text, or an hour on another. There is no way I've found to predict these differences. But they are revealed almost as soon as you start to rehearse.

I have found it counterproductive, not to say frustrating, trying to bend this rhythm to some outside sense of time. Going too fast OR too slow through the material are equally dissatisfying. Again, what is needed is balance. Don't be intractable about time. React to circumstances. If you've done all you need to do on a scene, move on. Don't just keep running it for its own sake, just because the schedule says you have another half hour to work on it. Even taking an extended break might be more productive. Similarly, if you haven't finished with a certain scene to your satisfaction, don't move on just because the schedule tells you to. See if you can keep working on that scene and make up the time somewhere else or accept the fact that it's taking longer than expected and consult with the stage manager about adjusting the schedule accordingly. Let the material dictate the schedule as much as possible, within reason.

The schedule of rehearsal may well be somewhat fluid, and yet it needs to act as an anchor for the actors and the designers and production crews. Having an overarching sense of what you will be able to accomplish, and where you need to be by a given time, is essential. It is also vitally important to share that plan with everyone.

Let the actors know the plan. Listen to their feedback about the schedule, if they have any. If they know where the time is being spent, they can gauge their own pace which they'll need to build to an audience-ready performance.

Fringe and/or Indies

I have long wished for more flexible structures for rehearsals. The present structure as laid out in the Canadian Theatre Agreement sometimes feels like a race to the finish just to get the piece "ready" for public consumption. One hits the ground running, and you dare not slow down for fear of falling behind. No time for deep reflection, or to try different ideas, or to sit in confusion, or to risk not making decisions right away. The economics of traditional medium-to-large scale companies operating under union guidelines simply can't handle flexible structures.

Independent theatre or festivals such as the Fringe do and can offer artists some flexibility for one reason only: the pay ranges from minimal to none. Scheduling rehearsals must be flexible because often the participants must work in other jobs to pay their bills, and can only rehearse when available. This usually means that (hopefully) approximately the same number of hours will be spent rehearsing as for traditional companies, just way more spread out.

In these cases, careful and creative scheduling becomes even more important. It is too easy to become complacent, and to think that you have loads of time, because you may have weeks or even months before an audience arrives, but add up the rehearsal hours and see exactly how many real working hours are left to you, and try not to freak out. Of course, the advantage of working this way is that there is time between rehearsals to reevaluate what you've done as a director and to make adjustments, and for actors to do some considered homework, learn their lines, and really think about their role. Unfortunately, this time is also often shared with making a living.

I directed Judith Thompson's wonderful version of *Elektra* at Humber College, and for various reasons, we had to work two-and-a-half days a week spread over ten weeks of time. I jumped at the chance to work this way, and looked forward to the spaces between rehearsals for planning, imagining, and having room for creative problem-solving. But it was a severe adjustment to my habitual internal work clock. The students were busy with other classes during that time, and the assignments and deadlines associated with those classes. Often, when I've directed at colleges or theatre schools, all other class work is suspended during the rehearsal period, leaving the students to completely focus on the production I was directing. Suddenly, I was confronted with a momentum issue that I had never encountered before. It took a bit of time to catch up from the last time we had rehearsed, which of course is never a problem when working five or six full days a week. That said, my expectations of the thinking and research work from the students between rehearsals were high, and they responded well, so that when we came back to rehearsals, they were generally well prepared, armed with thoughts or questions about the scenes we were tackling that day. So, as in all things, there were both good and bad things in that structure, and I would love to work that way again.

Pressure

Economic realities tend to be intractable. Companies, no matter what their mandate, are looking for "successful" shows, in terms of both reception and ticket sales. I have been involved in shows that were critically successful but drew poor numbers. I have done shows that were not well received by the press which sold out. I've done shows I was extremely proud of about which very few people I trust shared my opinion. And vice versa.

It's hard to quantify success. Or failure. But still, there is pressure to produce "success." This is pretty antithetical for an art form that is singularly process-driven. Most importantly, you can't create art whose goal is success. That just produces bad art and doesn't work anyway. There is a serendipity to success that can't be predicted or planned for. Your work will connect with audiences or it won't. You can only be true to your process, your collaborators' processes and what you are trying to say, and success will follow. Or it won't. Resist the need to "succeed." It will not help you or your collaborators.

The End Game

Hopefully, towards the end of the period in the rehearsal hall, there is now more time to really go deeper, try new ideas, fine tune, rediscover, and generally do the exciting work that comes with a knowledge of the piece and the people doing it.

This might be a good phase in which to go back to the operative words. Mostly, I give this task as homework to be done by the actors just before previews. Review the words. Was the original choice of operative words strong? What is helpful in those choices? Are there now better choices now that they know the piece and their character better?

I also ask them to read the script again as if for the first time. Are they missing anything? Do they really have their lines memorized EXACTLY, including punctuation? Is the stage manager still giving line notes? Did an original impulse that they had when they first read the play get lost or was it reinforced? If so, is that a good or a bad thing?

Often, the first exercises are also good as the last.

9

Talking to Actors

Theatre is an actor's medium. Period.

With a camera, the director has significantly more control. They frame the shot, choose which takes they prefer, and we the audience experience the story through their lens. Literally. These and many other decisions, like how much time can be spent on how many takes, what is shot and how close, what ends up on the cutting-room floor, and the pace and focus of how the camera tells the story determine much of the actor's performance. True, great film actors understand the camera, and know how to let it reveal their innermost thoughts and emotions, but they must relinquish much of their work to the director.

Not so in theatre. Ultimately, it is the actor's communication with the audience that is at the heart of the art form. The director may make pretty pictures, pace a story excellently, cast superlatively, ratchet up the dramatic tension inexorably, and otherwise facilitate all the production elements into a finely honed and gripping time in the theatre, but without the actor's willingness, talent, skill, and passion to communicate the story to their audience live, and in the moment, it is all for naught.

I have a few rules (surprise surprise) on a director's communication with actors:

1) Model the behaviour you want.

2) Who cares whose idea is whose?

3) Resist making decisions too early.

4) Confront everything.

5) Remember, it is the actor who is doing it, not you.

Explanations:

1) If you want to be listened to, LISTEN. If you want respect, be respectful. If you want to engage in a meaningful dialogue with your collaborators, you must initiate and encourage that dialogue. Create the atmosphere you want by showing the way.

2) If you are so ego-driven as to have every idea be recognized as yours, you're either in the wrong profession, or you're an asshole, or both. Most actors commit to choices they initiate, or at least make collaboratively, far more fully than those that are imposed upon them. Theatre is a collaborative art form. COLLABORATE.

3) In many cases, it is not necessary for decisions to be made too soon. There can be learning opportunities in not knowing. Unless certain decisions affect other departments, leave your options open. Options are good. Embrace the chaos. But check to make sure that all the actors are comfortable with this way of working.

4) If you see an actor uncomfortable, or frustrated, or confused, or anything else that is not helpful, ask them what's wrong. It may be part of their process, and nothing is amiss. It may

have nothing to do with you or the production, in which case it's none of your business, unless they want to confide in you. But it may be that they need clarification, or encouragement, or another helpful thing that you can provide. The worst thing you can do is to pretend that it doesn't exist. This also applies to group dynamics that might be present. Solicit a response to any group subtext you feel is present and deal with it.

5) It only matters that the actor understands and can commit to the idea. As the director, it is *your* job to find the language or image that the actor understands. It is not up to the actor to try to decipher the words the director uses to communicate the intention. It is the director's responsibility to find the actor's language.

Another variation of the Over-Director and Non-Director are Dictatorial and Absent. Again, neither extreme is desirable.

O O O

Barbara Coloroso, the parenting guru, talks about two kinds of parents: Jell-O and brick wall. Jell-O parents are totally *laissez-faire*. Anything goes. There is no structure, no routine, no clarity, no limits. Brick wall parenting, on the other hand, is rigid and unbending. There is no room for flexibility or spontaneity. Children obey the rules, because they are afraid to break them. Obviously, a balanced combination of the two — called backbone parenting — is more desirable. Children need to be encouraged to think for themselves. They have a responsibility for their own care. There is structure, there are boundaries and limits and codes of behaviour, but there is also flexibility and space and time to play.

O O O

Now, obviously, actors are not children and directors are not parents. But as a parent of four children myself, I have found that the times I can see my children as equal partners in their own upbringing, and behave accordingly, are the times that I am most successful at it.

I sometimes feel the title itself is open to misleading assumptions. "Director" implies a hierarchical relationship to those that would be "directed" (the verb comes from the Latin "to make straight"!). Most often, the director is a fulcrum, or hub of others' work. They are a guide, a focus from which the world of the production emanates. Unless the complete process is a collective creation in which all the participants have an equal say, from the initial ideas to the last performance of the run, then there needs to be a final arbiter for decision-making. In these situations, the director is granted an authority as an outside eye.

Most actors want and need structure. There needs to be *context* for their work. Their work needs to co-exist with their fellow actors' work. They need a world in which their choices and ideas make sense. They need feedback as to how their work is heard, seen and understood by the audience-to-come. They are not puppets, or tools, or vessels, or anything existing only to further the director's "vision." They are artists looking for truth and power in their work. They are equal participants in the creation of the production, but do not have responsibilities that require an objective perspective or anyone else's work but their own. How can they? They are inside the process and have a unique perspective that the director doesn't have, just as the director has an outside eye/ear/brain that the actor doesn't have. The relationship is symbiotic, not hierarchical.

This all may sound platitudinous, but it is surprising how few processes are satisfying to actors. Many feel the need to "director-proof" their process — a term I loathe — so as not to lose their way in the creation of their own work. As much as I hate the phrase, I do understand the sentiment. When I work as an actor, I often feel like I have to do my own homework in a vacuum, because the director is either not doing any investigative work on their own, or not doing any with the actors, or alternatively, trying to impose their will on the cast.

That is why actors take to the text methodology as described in Part 1 so readily. That is why treating actors with respect, and listening to their problems, their ideas, and their preferred ways of working are so important. Actors shouldn't feel the need to "director-proof" themselves — working separately from and in spite of the director — but rather choose to collaborate and trust that their director wants what's best both for the production and their role in it, and by working with them, their work will be clearer, deeper, and more focused.

But the director must earn that trust.

Creating Atmosphere

Why do we subject ourselves to committing to this ridiculous art form? The pay is usually awful. There is little opportunity for individual recognition, especially in Canada. As Sara Botsford once said, "There IS a ladder of success in Canada. It's just lying on the ground." Collaborations can be hit or miss. New plays may be exciting, but they are risky, because usually they are not given sufficient time or resources to gestate fully.

We rack our brains; why did we first want to do it? Why did we fall in love — or at least, in love/hate — with the art form?

I personally think there is only one real answer: because it was FUN. At its best, theatre practice is playful, silly, challenging, and infuriating, but it must be fun, or else, why bother?

The best rehearsal atmospheres often feel like an "us vs. the world" mentality. We understand our own specific difficulties because we are part of this gang, trying to put together a show that the public may or may not appreciate, or understand, or be moved by. We are all in this together. We feel safe to take risks, to be goofy, to be open, to reveal secrets when appropriate, to share ourselves, and to listen. Always to listen.

Again, modelling is the key for the director. And you need to have a sense of humour if you want your cast and crew to have fun. Lighten up. Almost always, if the cast doesn't enjoy working on the play, the audience will not enjoy witnessing it. Fun is infectious. Commitment is palpable. In the same way that a director models behaviour, and by extension, atmosphere, so too does a cast communicate their fun and commitment to the material when they perform to an audience.

Actors and Design

Sometimes, it is advantageous to have actors involved in certain design decisions, especially if those decisions directly affect them. The most obvious have to do with costume. The actor must feel good about the clothes they are wearing, both from a comfort point of view as well as for their character choices. Obviously, their input must be in line with the world the designer and director have conceived. Important personal props may also be helpful to have the actor's input. Their opinions may be invaluable, both to them as well as to the production as a whole. Again, specificity is all.

If it seems appropriate, I will also get an actor's opinion on sound cues.

> I was directing Diane Flacks' play *Waiting Room*, and Ari Cohen was playing a doctor who was afflicted with early onset Alzheimer's. Every so often, the character would have an episode of extreme disorientation, accompanied by sounds and lights. During the technical rehearsals, Ari was having trouble connecting to the sounds that were supposed to emanate from his brain. He asked for certain other sounds to be used, which seemed totally reasonable to me, and which the sound designer was able to accomplish fairly easily.

Sometimes, however, actors are unable to separate their inner life from the theatrical expression of that image or to experience what the audience experiences.

In the same production, the actors expressed concern over the last music cue, which was supposed to be beautiful, powerful and ultimately redemptive. They felt the cue wasn't building to a strong enough climax at the end. I assured them it was. Before the last dress rehearsal, I had the cast sit in the auditorium to hear the cue. What they couldn't hear was that as the music built, the sound travelled from the back of the stage towards the auditorium, building inexorably towards a powerful conclusion for the audience. On stage, they heard the sound lessening. The audience heard an inexorable build. The cue was amazing, designed and performed by the brilliant Reza Jacobs. As they heard it from the audience, they all uttered, "Ohhhhh," realizing that the cue was for the audience, and not for them. But the fact that I took the time to play it for them was vitally important — to me and to them.

Often, young directors become stressed because they feel that every idea and every inspiration must come from them. They feel that everyone is looking to them for all the answers at all times. The above story can be interpreted in different ways. Some directors would feel it was a form of mutiny by the actors to be expressing concerns about a design decision. But I think that actors feeling so invested in the production that they want every moment to be as good as it can be is an asset that is literally invaluable.

By concentrating on questions and not answers — at least at the beginning — and by genuinely collaborating with one's co-creators, not only is the pressure removed from the director to always be brilliant and "right," but the work will be more interesting, and the team will be more engaged and creative.

Your collaborators will sense that you will always have ideas and strong opinions when none other are present, or when there is the need for a focus (direction) of the discussion to "point the way" as a guide. Take control when necessary, but never be unnecessarily controlling.

What's Important?

Beware of power struggles. Avoid them whenever possible.

Some actors like to challenge the assumed authority of a director. They want to see how far they can go in proving the director has no idea of what they're talking about. It may be because these actors have been burnt so often in the past by Over-Directors or Non-Directors that they want to know how much they're going to have to do themselves. It could be a reaction to feeling powerless. It could be for myriad reasons. Even more frustrating for me is the actor who abdicates all responsibility of choosing possible paths of exploration, and when asked a question, replies, "You're the director. You tell me what you want and I'll do it."

Thankfully, these power struggles are few and far between in my experience. What's important is not to get sucked into that energy. They are lose/lose scenarios. And if no one else, the director must always be the adult in the room.

Just like in any other interpersonal relationship, many times what the struggle is about is either totally inconsequential and quickly unremembered, or really about something else, such as a tone of voice, a perceived bit of subtext, or something in the actor's past. Like Rule #4 in Talking to Actors (Confront Everything), it is important to deal with it, but make sure to create a private space to do it. Again, maybe it has nothing to do with you.

> I directed the late and wonderful actor Peter Donaldson in Michael Healey's *Plan B* at the Tarragon Theatre in 2002. I was working on a particular monologue with him, and he seemed to be rolling his eyes at every suggestion I made, or otherwise dismissing any help I was trying to offer. Finally, because he was the only actor in the room, I asked if I was bugging him. Did he hate my ideas? Was I hindering his process rather than helping?

He became quite contrite, and explained he was always like this in rehearsal. He insisted he liked my ideas. It was, he said, because he hated acting. "I'd much rather be gardening, or playing golf, or doing almost anything besides this." "Why the hell are you an actor, then?" I asked him. "Because I'm unqualified to make a living any other way." he replied. We got on really well after that, and he deservedly received a Dora nomination for his performance.

Now, sometimes, the power struggle may be about the tiniest moment that pretty well no one will notice one way or another. Yes, the devil is in the details, but some details are not worth arguing about. If there is more to be gained by letting an actor have their way, at least in the short term, LET IT GO! Don't let the power struggle overtake the general atmosphere in the room or poison the relationship between you.

Later, if you strongly feel that their way of playing that moment distracts from the ultimate purpose of the moment, scene or performance, then you can renew the discussion. But the actor is much more likely to listen and give up their idea now that they've had a really good shot at doing it their way.

Creating Individual Relationships

It is vital to have unique and individualized relationships with each and every actor in the cast. Different actors need different help at different times. Not all words make sense to all actors. Some actors like to be pushed hard, others less so.

Again, this may seem obvious, but it is surprising how many directors don't practise these guidelines. They assume that actors will be receptive to the director's language. "Why should I change my language and tailor it to different actors?" they think. "I'm the director. Let the actor adapt to me."

This is ridiculous. Again, it is the actor who is doing the storytelling, not the director. The director is giving the context, not the text. Your job is to help the actor, not bend them to your will, or reproduce a performance that you have imagined in great detail in your mind.

I try to establish individual relationships early on and have them develop throughout the process. Often, I will talk privately with an actor, going off to a corner of the rehearsal hall to speak apart from the rest of the cast. This creates a relationship in discussing things that no one else needs to hear. This is different from shared knowledge such as what happens in the text work. Those discussions are about content, story and meaning. These discussions deal directly with the actor's ability to execute or interpret often difficult or subtle colours in performance.

Separating the Actor and Their Work

Actors are notoriously vulnerable. And for good reason. They are their instrument: their body, their voice, their imagination. Their very presence and personality are the tools they use to create their art. If they are criticized for their technique, it's personal — literally. If praised, it is as if they are being celebrated as a human being, not just as an artist.

It is important to separate the artist from their craft. In other words, if the director remarks on what they see at a given moment, rather than how the actor is doing at that moment, it is much less intimidating or potentially hurtful. For instance, after a scene or a moment is played, the director might say, "Okay, so I saw that you were somewhat put down by the other character in that pass, and so your character seemed to wilt under the pressure. Is this what we want here?" rather than, "Come on! Don't be a wimp. Stand up to them. Don't let them win here!" The first is about the choice, the second is more personal and judgmental of their behaviour. The line between the character and the actor can be thin. Direction can be heard as a criticism of the person, rather than a conversation about the work.

Most every actor craves honest feedback. But what the director should be feeding back is the work — the choice of how something is being communicated — rather than something which can be seen as a value judgment about the choice itself.

It's a classic situation when a director says, "This is what I got from you during that bit," and the actor says, "Really, that's not what I was intending." The actor may not know how their character is being perceived, which is not necessarily a bad thing. A far worse situation would be an actor trying for an effect or a result, rather than just playing the intention. This is where the director helps, by being the mirror to the actor's choices.

Sometimes, I may not be sure if the actor is intentionally doing something which is good or is randomly playing something they're not fully aware of. In this case, I'll say, "You're doing this already, but I just want to make sure that this is where we're headed here." I do this because there is nothing worse than a director giving the actor a direction on something that they're already doing. It almost feels like theft, or at least as if they are trying to take credit for something the actor has initiated.

Once again, language is all important in the director's communication. We all know that one word or phrase can make all the difference, either positively or negatively. My career is littered with harmful, limiting, stupid, or confusing things that directors have said to me.

Unhelpful Directions:

I was once told by a director to make what was happening in the scene "more blue." Totally confused, I asked them, "By that, do you mean 'sad'?" They replied angrily, "No! More blue! More...blue!" I responded that I didn't know what they meant. The playwright, who was present, said, "You don't want the other guy to leave the room." "Oh," I said, "I can play *that*."

I was once told by a director, just after the dress rehearsal the night before our first preview, that they liked everything I was doing, but there was "something missing" from my first scene. They couldn't put their finger on it, but something was definitely missing. I spent a sleepless night, rethinking every line, every moment of that first scene. I finally hit on a possible idea. The next day, I went to the director and asked if that was what was missing. They replied, "No, don't worry about it. I was just upset about something else. The scene is great. Don't change anything." I was tired and cranky for my first preview.

I was once told by a director that my performance was quite good, but then they said, "I probably should never say this to an actor, but now all you have to do to make it great is to be funnier." We started working again, and everything I was doing was reduced to rat shit as I was, rather self-consciously, trying to "be funnier." Finally, I stopped rehearsals and said, "You're right. You should never say that to an actor!"

Directors often don't know to separate the intention from the effect. It can be frustrating and ineffective for an actor to be told only about the effect one's performance is creating rather than dealing with the intention. The director must bridge these two aspects: helping the actor with their objectives, subtext, backstory, and inner psychology, and reflecting back to them how that intention is being realized, including characterization, pace, staging, and size of performance. These two aspects (sometimes described as the inner and the outer) are inextricably linked, but they should be clearly delineated so the actor knows exactly what a given problem may be and begin to figure out how to solve it.

The inner work needs to find its way to the outside world, and be clearly and strongly executed. But notes purely about the effect their work is having can produce a self-consciousness in the actor that can be debilitating.

Fear

Most actors hang on every word a director says. Some directors, who have never or rarely acted, don't realize this. They confuse the performance bravura that most actors possess with self-confidence. Others, who are actors, forget this when they direct. But we all know how insecure the activity of being in front of an audience is. This is not self-indulgence. It is just, by definition, fucking scary.

This fear has — at least — two facets: the fear of being in front of an audience when you don't really know what you're doing, and the fear of delving into emotionally murky waters and dwelling in those ugly places for the life of the run. The better and deeper the work, the scarier it is. Courage, whether in battle, in interpersonal relationships, or on stage, is being scared and still going ahead and doing the thing that scares you. Most actors are extraordinarily brave.

Some directors fear this bravery. Some resent it. Some just can't fathom why a person would subject themselves to this fear. Good directors acknowledge the fear, and help the actor embrace it. They recognize that it is an essential part of the process and the cost of doing what we do. The worst thing would be to pretend it doesn't exist, or to dismiss it.

Where the director truly earns their money is in helping actors who are adrift and are needing help to find their way. It is much easier working with those who have been on top of the character and their choices from Day 1. Searching for the right keys, instilling confidence, and liberating the imagination are the antidotes to the fear of not knowing what you're doing.

Actors know that there can be emotional and physical fallout in doing good work. Somehow and for some unknown reason, we still think it's worth it. In order to achieve truly deep work, the actor must approach that place of fear and confront it, and ultimately never forget it. It is a fine line between succumbing to the fear and channelling it to create true stage magic. Perhaps that's why some actors are so emotionally fragile, have substance abuse issues, or like to live on the edge. I like to believe that we're getting better at separating ourselves from the work, but it's an ongoing struggle for many actors.

Here are some things said by directors that resonated with me, mostly given as general notes to the entire cast after a run-through:

Helpful Directions:

"You've done your homework, so leave it at home. It's for you, not the audience. You don't need to prove that you're a conscientious actor."

"Listen. Don't show that you're listening, just listen. And if you're aware that you're listening, stop, and just listen."

"You don't need to cry to get the audience to be moved. Sometimes it is far more emotionally effective for an audience to see a character trying desperately not to cry than actually seeing tears on their face."

Previews

Clearly, the number of previews you have will determine how much work can or should be done.

Traditionally, you have a five-hour call during the day before a preview to work. You might want to make changes to staging, technical cues, transitions or other elements that can be altered. If it's a new play, there might be cuts, rewrites, or even additions if deemed necessary. You might want to take a fresh look at a few scenes, or even just moments; to go deeper, to pick up the pace, or to get the actors to listen better. But there is a danger of overburdening the actors with changes when they are still in the process of finding their footing.

I find that whatever can be fixed with a note might be more desirable than re-rehearsing something over and over, which can deflate energy and confidence, unless requested by the actor/s. Audience reactions are now part of the equation, but sometimes it is a mistake to generalize too much about their reactions, such as the frequency and intensity of laughs, the attention span in certain moments, or the overall effect the play is generating based on just a few performances. There is value in letting the actors go for a bit and giving them space to find their way.

Partially what is being developed during previews is the process that will continue throughout the run after opening. Will there be a strong sense of communication between the cast members? Is their individual and collective commitment to the story being maintained or even increased? Is there a consistency in the performance that still leaves room for appropriate spontaneity?

As I've mentioned in many other places in this book, the balance is all. Work by all means, but don't overwhelm them with too many significant changes. If reworking a scene, leave it on a positive note, so that they can look forward to performing it that night. If it's a new play, don't ask an actor to learn huge amounts of new text and expect them to perform it in a few hours in front of a paying audience. And as always, solicit the actors' feedback on how much they can take and how much they can't.

Giving Notes

Note sessions to me are always best in person and all together. As an actor, I hate receiving notes via email or even on a piece of paper or via the stage manager, except for line notes. Usually note sessions happen after a run-through of a section, or of the whole play. As a director, always make time for notes after these runs, and if you can't, start the next day with them. Note sessions are a time for everyone to connect, to reflect together, and to be reminded of our common purpose.

General notes to the whole group are invaluable to inspire, to reignite commitment, to encourage discussion if appropriate, to continued exploration, to going deeper, and to remind everyone of basic tenets, such as "being there" or listening. General notes reiterate why we are doing this play, what's important to remember going forward, and what the touchstones are of our production, both in content and in form.

Specific notes should be liberating, not inhibiting. If they are part of an ongoing private conversation you have with an actor, it's not bad to begin to share some of that information with the rest of the group. Very often, as I might be giving a specific note to a specific actor, I might open it up and tell everyone that the same note could also equally apply to them.

Obviously, specific notes should never blame, shame or single out an individual for criticism. Again, not only are there ethical issues which make those actions heinous, but it's an ineffective tactic. Actors (i.e. human beings) tend to do their best work when they feel supported and encouraged.

The best note sessions make the actors want to go out and do the show again. They should energize, not deflate. They should inspire.

10

—

...And Others

Adding Tech — Transitions/Scene Changes

As I mentioned previously, I start working on the transitions from the very beginning of my staging work, especially if the actors are mainly doing them. They are part of the movement, the pace, the content and the feel of the story. They are opportunities, and shouldn't be seen as problems or any kind of necessary evil.

As you add lights and sound to them, be aware of how visible you wish them to be, how stylized or purely functional, and how they can relieve or build dramatic tension.

In *Detaining Mr. Trotsky* at the old Toronto Free Theatre, I had a scene change happen while dialogue with two actors were downstage, isolated in a spotlight. Upstage and not really visible, the actors changed the scene. At a certain point, one of the downstage actors turned to speak to someone else in the scene upstage, and the lights snapped into next state, and we were "magically" in the new location, without pause.

Another time, in one of the few musicals I have ever directed (Jim Betts' *Colours in the Storm*), I choreographed a musical number at the end of a scene as the scene change, so that when the song was over, we were already in the next location.

Daniel Brooks' transitions in his production of *Half Life* by John Mighton were slow moving, beautiful, dance-like...almost soulful, and communicated an atmosphere that totally enhanced the nature of the play's ideas and its storytelling. I remember them as strongly as I do the wonderful performances as an aspect of the powerful story.

The word "transition" (a much better term than "scene change") literally means to "go across" — time, space, mood, conceptual ideas? — it could be any or all of these, but the key is the word "go." It is active.

Paper Techs

It's always helpful to start to incorporate the technical elements (except the lights, which is usually impossible and impractical to achieve) in the rehearsal hall as much as possible. Having even a rough version of the sound and/or video cues will save time and frustration later, especially for the stage manager, who will be rehearsing the timing and getting to know the intention of the cues. However, sometimes this may not be possible.

In these cases, it is extremely advisable to have paper techs with your designers along with your stage manager before you begin working these elements in the theatre. For those who don't know, a paper tech is when the director and the above designers consider where they imagine there will be cues and discuss their basic concept and function, as the stage manager puts those cues in their prompt book. Just knowing where you envision the cues will be helpful to all concerned and will undoubtedly save time during the level sets and cue-to-cues.

What gets decided during a paper tech is not set in stone. Cues will probably get cut or added once the technical side of the production and the performance of the actors start to unite into one organism. But it's always helpful to have a starting point from which to build the look and feel of the world we are all trying to create.

Running Level Sets / Cue-to-Cues / Tech Rehearsals

Your set is built, although it may not be totally finished. Costumes will follow soon. The props are standing by, waiting for the actors to use them. It's time for your level sets.

In the U.S., they don't have a separate session to set lighting states without actors. I have never understood this. Maybe it is because I'm used to working the way we do in Canada. We use the lighting level session with light walkers as an opportunity for me and the lighting designer to "paint" our production and decide on where and how to focus the audience's attention. It allows us to take our time to get it right. That said, it is important not to over-dwell on a lamp level or fade count. These sessions are the first draft. Adjustments will undoubtedly be made later, in the context of the actors actually being present.

Although I get the concept of the American position — that it seems too "theoretical" to build the states without actors — it is extremely hard on the performers to just be light walkers — usually for two or three long days — and not a particularly good use of their time. Better they have that time off (usually a day, or even just a couple of mornings) to learn lines, run bits by themselves, or rest, rather than the exhausting task of endlessly waiting while the lighting states are being built. And when they do finally get on stage, most of the cues will already be in the lighting board.

I like to have a day on stage with the actors without tech. This gives the actors a chance to get used to the actual set in the space instead of the tape on the floor of the rehearsal hall. There's time for trying out the acoustics. Get the actors to sit in the audience to listen to each other, hearing just how loud their voices and how precise their diction must be. Entrances and exits can be finely timed, backstage tracks can be tried, props placements and any other spacing requirements, both offstage and onstage, can be finalized. Most importantly, the transfer from rehearsal to performance space is beginning. The energy and size of the performances often need a bit of a boost now, especially in larger theatres. How can you keep the intensity and subtlety you had in the hall, and still make sure that everything is clearly audible for the audience? And oftentimes the spacing might need to change. What seemed perfect in the hall might need to be enlarged or shifted. The sightlines will almost certainly need to be checked and rechecked. In short, this day in the space without tech is invaluable to solve myriad problems.

Now, even though you might have had separate level sets without the actors for lights, sound and video if being used, and any other relevant element, the cue-to-cue with actors will still be long and taxing. As the director, you will be juggling several balls at once. You must figure out which elements may need adjustment in a specific sequence and be clear about why and how they need changing. Resist being dictatorial but be clear as to what you want and why. Check in with your designers. Be flexible enough to listen to their input but know where your production lives. Be ready to make strong decisions when needed. Trust your instincts and don't second-guess yourself. No decision on a cue is irrevocable.

Decisions made in cue-to-cue will often need adjusting when you see the whole piece in the context of a run, so don't spend too much time on any individual cue or sequence of cues. The beautifully moody lighting cue that everyone loved in the level set may not be what the story needs at that point.

I directed a production of George F. Walker's brilliant play *Zastrozzi* for Penguin Theatre in Ottawa in the early '80s. I had several meetings with George before I went, asking questions about certain aspects of the text. As I left our last meeting on my way to drive to Ottawa, George yelled down the street after me. "Remember," he said, "it's a comedy!" Cut to four weeks later, after a dress rehearsal that seemed to be dragged down in a mire of atmospheric gloom, I finally heard George's voice in my head. I turned to the lighting designer and asked that all the cues be made brighter. Comedy needs light. The play sang after that.

Make certain that the decisions are still directly related to the content of your story and the way you've decided to tell it. Like comedy without substance — or for that matter, anything without substance — you need more than just the image. You need *context*.

And don't forget the actors! Just because you're mainly concentrating on the technical elements does not mean that there aren't opportunities to have private conversations on a moment or scene, to suggest other acting choices, or otherwise continue your ongoing dialogue with your actors. Get them to use the time for themselves, running lines, rehearsing bits (unobtrusively), or being otherwise engaged. All time is precious. Don't waste any.

Or get them to watch some of the cues. It's the only time they'll probably get to see how it looks from the audience.

Your Stage Manager

Often the most underrated member of the team.

The stage manager is your partner. They are your surrogate when you're not there. There needs to be trust — on both sides. A good relationship with your stage manager is essential. It is as important to choose the right stage manager as it is your actors.

I need the stage manager to understand the priorities of the production, and to be as committed and excited as I am about the nature of our artistic goals. They should have a good and honest relationship with each individual actor as well as the production departments based (ideally) on mutual trust and respect. I also want them to understand the inherent rhythm of the piece, which will inform how they call the technical cues.

They are also Head Timekeeper. When you make the daily schedule with your stage manager, get their opinion about how long certain scenes might take. Discuss what will happen if things take more or less time than allotted. Have Plans B and C in your pocket. So, when you're working away and the stage manager gently reminds you that you have five minutes left to work on this scene, you will be able to refer to a pre-discussed option.

That said, when it's time to take a break, or break for lunch or finish at the end of the day, those limits are intractable. They are NOT inhibitors of creativity. They are negotiated agreements that were hard fought for and must not be abused. Never take advantage of an actor's willingness to keep working longer than the prescribed working hours. They and you might want to, but it is just wrong to do it.

I rely on the stage manager to communicate clearly with everyone involved in the production and for sage and sober advice; on feedback of how rehearsals are going; on scheduling issues, on the organization of backstage, on morale, and to provide any information that might be useful to our process. It's a lot to ask of one person. But then again, the theatre demands a lot.

Technicians

There are two types of directors (heard this before?) in terms of how they work with technicians; those who involve these artists/artisans in the process and treat them as knowledgeable craftspeople, and those that see them as minions to do their bidding.

More often than not, a director has little to do with the carpenters, paint crew, props persons, costumers, lighting/sound/video operators, etc., before moving into the theatre and starting technical rehearsals. If possible, I always find it helpful to at least meet these essential collaborators and learn their names. This may sound obvious or banal, but it is surprising how many directors don't practise this most basic politeness. And it might have the added benefit of providing goodwill from the crew that will hopefully go the extra mile for you and your show.

It is vital that you create a strong relationship with the lighting, sound and any other operators of the production. They need to understand the nature and feel of the show, and not just press a GO button while streaming a video or reading a book. Try to inspire them as to why we're all doing this piece. Hopefully, your stage manager will be extremely helpful with this, as they will have the ongoing relationship with the operators after opening when you have left.

A lot of technicians have a very sensitive "bullshit meter." They may have been burned by Over-Directors or even Abusive Directors who treated them like crap or even ignored them completely. Never forget your sense of humour. Don't take yourself or your show so seriously as to lose sight of the fact that this profession is supposed to be fun. You can be demanding but still be polite and pleasant to work with.

The Production Manager/Technical Director

Similarly, you want the production manager (P.M.)and/or the technical director (T.D.)to feel a sense of ownership for the project. Don't treat them like they are your underlings. Again, asking questions can be way more effective than making demands: "Is this possible?" rather than "I need this now!"

Most P.M.s and T.D.s want to help. They chose to work in theatre for many of the same reasons we all did, choosing to earn less money and work longer hours than if they did similar work in other fields.

If a P.M. complains that an idea is too costly, ask their advice about how we can achieve something similar within our budget. If a

T.D. insists that a given effect or piece of technology is beyond our means, ask their advice as to how we still can get what we would all want to produce top-quality storytelling. Present the problem and listen to their ideas. Then the discussions can be respectful and have a far greater chance of success.

> Yes, sometimes there will be conflict. I have been known, in a fit of pique, to take out my chequebook and write a cheque to guarantee that we would have funds to cover a back-up audio show tape (this was in the Jurassic Era when we still used analog tape...and cheques!). The P.M. in question, who I had nicknamed Dr. No, and I had a disagreement about whether the budget could handle this modest expense. In a production meeting, we shouted at each other as I wrote the cheque, throwing it down on the table, which he promptly tore up, saying, "I don't want your fucking money!" By the way, he was a brilliant production manager whom I continue to admire.
>
> This was NOT the way you should handle conflict. I was much younger and way more hot-headed. I got what I needed, but at the expense of bad feelings. I would handle this situation much better now.

The Artistic Director/Producer

The A.D./Producer has every right to give feedback to what they see and hear and experience about your work.

When I first started directing, I would become quite defensive about this input. My default reaction was to think that they didn't trust my talent or my judgment, that they were trying to put *their* stamp on *my* show. But in some way, shape or form, they are facilitating this production — usually financially — so their reactions deserve to be listened to. Hopefully, this discussion can be had in the context of them saying, "This is my suggestion, take it or leave it as you see fit." But it doesn't always work that way.

Disagreements will occur. Tastes vary. Priorities may be different. However, resist drawing your line in the sand unless you feel like you finally and absolutely have no choice. You can always listen carefully and consider the feedback, and then, after due consideration, if you don't want to follow the suggestion or you disagree with the assessment, you can have the debate. But you must be articulate and respectful about the disagreement, or else it becomes a power struggle, and nobody will truly win that fight.

Besides, they may be right. Or at least partially so.

If I strongly disagree with some feedback, I try to understand the source of where the observation is coming from. It might be that the suggestion of how to solve a particular problem is off base, but maybe the reason behind it is somewhat accurate. It might be that the tone of how the feedback was given is unhelpful, in which case you can be the grown-up and try to decipher what is behind their note. There might be some truth to it, but they might not be artists themselves and so not know how to "fix" a given problem or even how to communicate it. Or if they are artists, they might be trying to solve an issue as they would if it were their production.

> I once had a general manager of a company giving me notes about how the writer should rewrite their play, complete with some suggestions of dialogue. I explained to them that they were not the writer. If they had an issue with a section or passage, they could express their concern, and leave it at that, trusting that we would take their feedback seriously. They replied that in the administrative world, they would expect solutions to be offered, not just problems. I explained that was not the case in the creation of art.

Most people feel respected if they are heard. LISTEN to what they have to say, consider it, and adapt it or follow the advice if useful. But if it is not, be clear as to why it's not right for your show. Then the A.D./Producer will feel that they have been respected, their suggestion seriously contemplated, and their input valued. Chances are they will be satisfied with that no matter the decision.

11

After Opening

How much can you do after opening? Not much, according to our union and traditional structures.

It's ironic that after the most important element has been added — the audience — the work has been declared, for the most part, over. Yes, you can give a limited number of notes, and yes, actors, or at least good hardworking actors, try very hard each and every performance to create anew the choices that have already been made; to organically grow in their performance to incorporate new impulses and/or give life to spontaneous ideas that make themselves known. But the actual creation of the production, including the execution of the design, the staging, the technical choices and the general performance options are basically finished. For better or for worse.

The Director's Contract Only Goes Until Opening!

It is also ironic that the director's job is supposedly done after the official opening of the show; you usually receive your final payment on opening. It can be an emotional time for many directors, letting go of an entity that you have been with so intimately for so long, and be, for all intents and purposes, shut off from any continued work or growth it undertakes. To continue with the parenting analogy, it is rather like watching your child grow to maturity and leave home to follow their own life.

So, this is where that important relationship with your stage manager really comes to the fore. They are the guardian. Hopefully, they fully understand where the production lives as a whole, and how all component parts fit together. Hopefully, they understand each actor's journey and each actor's process, so that they can facilitate their growth during the run. They need to be able to differentiate between appropriate improvement and irrelevant or unsuitable change. They should be able to write good comprehensible show reports, so that it is clear how the show is evolving over the run. The best reports make you feel like you were actually at the show. The worst are a couple of generic lines that really tell you nothing.

But arguably, even more important is the task of giving notes to actors after opening, which falls to the stage manager (S.M.). This is an incredibly delicate responsibility, and one that many stage managers despise. Some just won't give actors any notes unless they are purely technical, such as, "You're a little too far right to be in your light." The best stage mangers are able to have a discussion with an actor if they feel that performance is starting to move off the rails in some way. I try to be clear with the cast that the S.M. has my complete confidence, but even so, some actors do not like being given notes by a surrogate. I always make sure that I am always available to consult with the S.M. if they have any issues, or if they feel I should see the show myself.

How Often Should You Go to the Show after Opening?

Obviously, some of this depends upon the length of the run, or whether the director is from out of town. I especially try to stay away as long as I can possibly manage just after opening, to give everyone a little room to breathe and not feel like I'm hovering, waiting to pounce with notes.

If it is a relatively long run — say five weeks or longer — I will often not return for about ten days or so. If a shorter run — say two weeks — I won't come for several days. After that, I will not appear too often — no more than once a week in the longer run — partially because I get frustrated that I can't change anything major at this point. When I do give notes, I try to be judicious, only giving ones that are absolutely important and easily executed. Again, it is vital to identify what is truly worth mentioning and what isn't. Unless a certain change affects the story or an image which reveals the story, let it go. If an actor wants to sit in a different place rather than the chair you had placed them in originally, does it really matter (unless of course they are not well lit in that new place)?

Reviews

It's taken me decades, but I never read reviews anymore when I am working as an actor; not even after the show has closed.

They are pernicious entities. A review is simply one person's opinion, and they may or may not be knowledgeable or even passionate about the art form. They will of course be opinionated, as all humans are, and might well be ill-disposed towards a type of theatre, its content, or even the personalities of the artists involved. It is, in short, a highly subjective reaction in an extremely public forum. I have never read a review that was helpful to my work. I have never read a review that made me feel my work was validated. I have never read a review that reflected my own assessment of my work or the piece as a whole. Worst of all are the comments on social media.

The biggest danger about reviews is that they might influence the actors' judgment of their work, and even, heaven forbid, start to change their performance. If the review is negative, it can totally deflate their confidence. If it is positive, it can give a false sense of accomplishment, or pit cast members against each other. As my ex-wife Kate Lushington has said, "Mistrust all reviews, especially the good ones."

The only time I read them now is when I'm directing a show and I hear that I may need to do damage control with the actors. I always encourage my cast not to read them, but it happens quite often that word will spread — through friends, social media, or the grapevine. As much as you tell a theatre company not to distribute them, they will most certainly use them — if they are favourable — in the lobby or in ads. Or they will choose the more positive selections if they're mixed. The theatre industry is very linked to reviews and extremely reliant on them as a marketing tool. And unfortunately, our fragile egos care.

It is difficult, but I still encourage my collaborators to resist reading this bane of our art form.

Remounts

Where some strong work can really happen is when there is a remount of the show that you have done previously. That's where one can go deeper and find more options than in the original incarnation. Not a surprise, since one is finally able to incorporate the audience's input into the equation. There might even be time or money to make design changes.

Actors redoing their original performance tend to be more relaxed and open. Directors can be focused on finding new, more complex and less obvious choices. All the artists will have time to address moments in the show with which they never felt happy. No one needs to worry if the show is viable. After all, if you're remounting it, it must have had something of worth to put it out there again.

Rounded Edges

This is what I call moments in a show — or even the whole piece — after some time has passed after opening.

As an actor, I know that when I first start performing in a new production, I am hyper-aware. I'm listening like crazy, unsure about the moment to come. I may not be totally comfortable with my dialogue. I may be unsure of certain moments, and how to make them better. I may not be sure about the effect the play is having in general. I am totally aware of my scene partner(s), because they're in the same boat as I am. We are all in a constant state of "being there," because we're not really sure where "there" is yet. In short, there are edges.

Then you open. It goes better than expected perhaps. Or perhaps even spectacularly. You're in a hit! Or at least what passes for a hit in Canada. Reviews are good, even though you try to never read them. People are buying tickets. Your friends and family really love it. Social media are burning up from all the "likes."

So, you can relax. You don't have to worry about whether or not the show works. It clearly does. You start trying to recreate moments you love or find new ones so that you can love *those* moments. The pace of the performance picks up, because now you really know your lines, and you're anticipating the sections of the show that work, that get big laughs, or in which you feel comfortable. You're confident in your fellow actors. They're great and open and present, and they too are more comfortable now. The show is getting SMOOTH. The edges are being sanded, because now you all know what you're doing most of the time. You are less hyper-aware. In short, you stop totally showing up.

> I believe it was David Mamet who said, "The actor's job is to show up." I think he's talking about REALLY showing up; being present and aware of everything, from your own state of readiness, to the material you're interpreting, to your fellow castmates, and to the audience. Easily said, extraordinarily difficult to do.

Of course, it's worse if the show is not so wildly successful. If it's not as good as you think it should be, you're working overtime trying to make it better. You're working really hard, and not just by being there, but by trying to bend the performance to your will to *make* it work, or at least make it palatable. And if the show is really not good at all (your judgment, not anyone else's), you're lucky if you're able to show up at all.

So, What the Hell Is "Showing Up"?

This is one of those conundrums that makes art in general, and the performing arts in particular, so frustrating and fascinating.

> The late great John Gielgud came and talked to my drama school. The thing I remember most about what he said was, "It took me until I was forty until I began to learn how to act, and until I was seventy until I learned how to do nothing."

Now that, as a performer, I'm approaching the "doing nothing" phase, I totally understand what he meant. It's about not having to prove anything. It's about trusting the audience to fill in certain blanks. It's about letting go of your own ego to allow the material to be front and centre, and not you, the interpreter of it. It's not about doing, it's about being.

o o o

A Zen proverb:

A wealthy person climbs a mountain, holding a fantastic gift for Buddha in each hand. They offer one. Buddha looks at it and says, "Drop it." They offer the second, and Buddha says, "Drop it." They offer both, and Buddha says, "Drop it." They think, and then do as Buddha says. They hold out their empty hands towards Buddha, and Buddha says, "Drop it."

o o o

Of course, "doing nothing" is not really doing nothing at all. You're doing a lot, but it just doesn't look like you are. If you are able to show up completely, if you've done all your homework, but are able to leave it behind where it belongs — at home and in the rehearsal hall — if you're truly listening, without indicating that you are, and if you're able to totally be in the present moment, not back in the one that has passed, nor anticipating the one yet to come, then you are beginning to approach "doing nothing."

> When Ted Dykstra and I were preparing to do *2 Pianos 4 Hands* for the first time, we both were suffering from tendonitis, as we weren't used to playing so much piano. We went to a brilliant physiotherapist at the Royal Conservatory of Music in Toronto. Time was getting very short, and we were getting very nervous. Whenever we made a mistake, we would both be really upset at ourselves. After several instances where we would swear and beat ourselves up for not being perfect, he said to us, "Once the note is played, it's gone forever." This is even more true for acting.

The above may sound pretty New Age or "woo-woo." I happen to think I am one of the least "spiritual" people on the planet, but this conundrum of doing nothing but everything, of being present but not showing you are, of showing up but not indicating that you're showing up, I know to be at the heart of great performing.

12

Director Training

I've left this subject for last because I believe that how and why directors are trained is still somewhat contentious.

Directing is a craft as much as an art, and there are techniques and tools that can be taught and practised within a training situation. For way too long, directors were assumed to simply emerge, coming from another branch of the theatre — usually actors, but not always — or from an academic institution.

Artistic choices are individual and are arguably unteachable. Where the artistic impulses come from, how they take shape, and how they then become a potential work of art is somewhat mysterious, instinctive, and certainly unique to each of us. I would never presume to tell another director what their choices should or shouldn't be.

But the process of communicating these choices to actors and other artists, and the techniques of collaboration, can and should be taught. Indeed, they must be taught. Young directors too often are thrown into the deep end, without enough analysis or practice in communicating with actors. These processes can always be deepened and refined with experienced directors as well. In the same way that art is an ongoing struggle to achieve excellence, so too is communication and collaboration a never-ending learning process.

Assistant Directing

I have always been of two minds about the benefits of assistant directing for aspiring directors.

It was never for me. As an actor, I feel like I was able to watch and witness a seasoned director working on a play in much the same way that an assistant might. It's true, I was not able to attend design or production meetings as an actor, but I often was hired as a musical director at the beginning of my career, and so I was able to be a part of the production team that way.

When I engage an assistant director who has requested to work with me, I warn them that I will probably not let them work on their own on any part of the production to test their skills, such as transitions, secondary rehearsals, or even line runs. For me, each of those aspects are vital parts of my production and its process, and I don't want to relinquish oversight of even the first pass of these activities.

I also ask that they not speak or contribute their opinions in rehearsal unless specifically asked. I find that too many voices in the rehearsal hall can be counterproductive. They are mostly there to observe, not necessarily to contribute. I do offer access to me at any time *outside* of rehearsal, and they can attend all meetings. I expect and encourage questions, opinions, suggestions and any other ideas as long as it is not in the hall. I will ALWAYS give them credit if I use an idea or suggestion that they have offered, and if they have shown intelligence, creativity, and sensitivity to the process, I might well solicit their voice later on in rehearsals. But that must be earned, and not automatically granted.

As you can tell, I'm not particularly generous with assistants.

Directing Student Actors

It may go without saying, but I'll say it anyway; working with student actors is significantly different than working with professionals. You are teaching as you direct. The main focus is NOT your brilliant production, but the learning process for the students. This applies to production and design students as much as acting students.

Now, I believe that the best learning environment will occur when I am directing much as I would in any situation, and work to create the best possible production possible. I ask for commitment, hard work, and engagement with the material. I expect that if a student doesn't understand something, that they will ask questions. And I make sure to model the behaviour I hope they will use when they graduate; politeness, respect, good listening skills, positive energy when working with others, and an insatiable drive for excellence.

The greatest difference when you are directing students is patience. Things you might have done often may be new for the student. Actors may not have much experience with heightened language, or stylized movement, or multitasking. Production students might be first-time stage managers, or lighting operators, or sound designers. Not ironically, by concentrating on a good learning process, the chances of a first-rate production being created are much greater.

Now, it might be somewhat more difficult when student directors are working with student actors and production or design students. There is an unspoken deference afforded a teacher/director that is absent when working with a peer. So, one needs to follow the modelling behaviour that much more rigorously. Listen. Be respectful. Work hard, but try to have fun. Don't take yourself too seriously. Recognize the unusual reality of the situation. Deal with issues as they arise, even if they're uncomfortable. Be confident without being arrogant. Be a leader without being controlling. And remember, everyone is learning as much as everyone else.

The Pedagogy of Director Training

Theatre schools need to commit to director training and be creative in how it's taught and, most importantly, by whom. Teachers may be wonderful educators, but not great practitioners. And vice versa. It is presumptuous in the extreme for any educator to dictate what directing is and how to do it. But skills and techniques may be taught, and experience at practising the art can be provided.

Now, before anyone jumps up and down and cries, "What about this book? Aren't you telling the reader what directing is?" I would reply that hopefully I am relaying my opinions and experience of what I believe about the craft, not prescribe anything about the art. In that vein, I believe:

1. Beginning directing students should be backstage crew, learn how to hang and focus lights, climb a ladder safely, be an assistant stage manager, paint a set or a wall or a floor, sweep and mop, and anything else that crews do. They need to understand every component that goes into making a production.

2. They should attend acting classes, including voice and movement, improvisation, and of course, scene study and rehearsals of a show.

3. They should be a part of a playwriting course, if there is one.

4. They need to learn how to research, and should begin acquiring an overview of world history, art history, theatre history, linguistics, and the social sciences.

Now, learning all these fields in any kind of depth is impossible in a short training program of two or three years. But at least the directing student should learn how to learn, where to go when researching a production, what research is useful and playable, and what isn't.

Most importantly, the directing student needs to direct. As much as possible. It would be ideal if they started with professional actors before being inflicted upon student actors. I have worked with directing students several times on scene study classes using seasoned actors, and the feedback provided to the students by the professional actors at the end of the course was an invaluable assessment of what was successful in the student's directing process and what needed more attention. Again, the focus is on the communication and execution of the ideas emanating from the student, rather than the ideas themselves.

There should be lots of other opportunities to direct as they continue their training, from site-specific venues, Theatre for Young Audiences material, classical texts and most importantly, new works, perhaps even acting as a dramaturg to student writers. That said, I think one needs to be careful not to leave the student writer and director to completely fend for themselves. They are both in the midst of a training process, and I would hate for a young director/dramaturg to guide a young writer to places they don't want or need or are able to go. Strong supervision should be present in these situations. In fact, every project the directing student undertakes should have a professional directing mentor.

More often than not, the greatest perceived lack of excellence in the theatre is the dearth of talented directors. It was not that long ago — about the beginning of the 20th century — that acting training first emerged. The training of technical skills, design, and even playwriting followed. Directing seems to be the last discipline of a considered, pragmatic pedagogy in the theatre. I think it's because theatre educators didn't see the way directors COULD be trained; that they somehow appeared magically, fully formed, from some cocoon somewhere.

But that's as ridiculous as believing that any artist doesn't need training, and that if they are truly special, they will find their way — somehow — and become the great artist they were always destined to be. The few that do appear in this way are the exception that proves the rule. For sure, some artists feel they don't need or want training, and they turn out well. But who knows how much better they might have been if they had trained?

My bias is clear.

PART THREE

—

NEW TEXT

13

Theatre for Young Audiences

I am, you might have gathered, a rather political animal. I grew up as what is known as "a red diaper baby"; my parents were Communists who left the party in 1956. Political thought and analysis were the very lifeblood of my family's makeup.

As I began my theatre training, and later, in my early career as an actor and director, I became more and more horrified as to just how elitist the art form is. Ticket prices are high in traditional regional and mid-sized theatres, not to mention exorbitant in larger and commercial theatres. Smaller independent theatres are usually sparsely attended. Only a relatively small ratio of the population attends the theatre at all.

There have also been cultural barriers. When I started out in the mid-1970s, the overwhelming majority of theatre artists were white, and people of colour were simply not represented in any real way on most stages in Canada. Therefore, it was not surprising that the vast majority of the audiences were white. Men ran these theatres in disproportionate numbers as compared to women, although more women attended theatre than men. These factors were not making any sense to my political agenda of using the art form to effect some kind of socio-political change. Thank goodness these conditions are finally changing.

Relatively early on in my career, I began to work in the Theatre for Young Audiences sector. Ironically, TYA is considered an "entry level" phase for the young professional. It is often thought of as a stepping-stone before "graduating" to adult theatre. In many ways, I think it should be the reverse. We should be graduating to TYA. For me, it is the most important theatre there is.

My belief is that TYA is the only real political theatre we have in Canada. Here's why:

1. It generally travels to its audience, rather than asking them to walk into a building that may feel alien to them. Although there is TYA that happens in traditional theatres, the type that usually excites me most are those that play in the home base of the young people. Therefore, you are playing to a true cross-section of the population.

2. Ticket prices are highly subsidized (and should be even more), and depending upon the government of the day, there might be significant incentives to provide schools with quality professional theatre, thereby removing any financial impediment.

3. Difficult and complex social issues are encouraged in its plays. School boards and teachers who wish for help in dealing with difficult subject matter appreciate having a play to refer to as a tangible teaching tool.

4. Most importantly, you are playing to an audience whose opinions are not yet entrenched. This audience is in the process of deciding what they think about themselves, the world, and their reactions to what they see around them.

There are many examples in my career in which I have witnessed young people who were deeply affected by shows on which I have worked. There is nothing more gratifying than to see an audience of young people laugh, be moved, or react with outrage — oftentimes vocally — at what they are experiencing. It is well known that you always know where you stand with this audience, as their reactions of engagement or boredom are clear and immediate. Here are three examples of the power of TYA:

I directed a high school piece by Dennis Foon called *Mirror Game*, in which a young woman is hit on several occasions by her boyfriend, after which he always apologizes profusely and begs for forgiveness, promising to never do it again. At every performance, the audience — mostly the female students — would scream at her not to take him back, groaning loudly when she did, and finally cheering when, towards the end, she doesn't.

David S. Craig's *Tough Case* introduced the concept and practice of restorative justice, and tells the tale of a young man who is convicted of vandalism, and who learns to accept responsibility for his actions and to make reparations to the victim of his crime. We toured to prisons as well as high schools, and during the talkback, a young prisoner tearfully revealed that they had wished they could have seen this play before they had committed their crime, for now, after seeing the play, they could appreciate the consequences of what they had done.

In Chris Craddock's play *The Incredible Speediness of Jamie Cavanagh*, the protagonist is a tween who suffers from ADHD. She is smart, kind, and imaginative, but has trouble concentrating in school, totally underachieves, and has little to no filter to think before she says some clever but rude remark which inevitably gets her in trouble. At the end of the show, the actress playing the part would be inundated with kids who wanted to share that they too were "like Jamie." They had never seen a story in which a person like them was the centre of the story.

Here was an area of theatre that made sense to me. Here was the kind of theatre that I could honestly say had the possibility of changing the world. About a third of the plays I have directed in my career have been in this field, almost all of which were original scripts.

Types of TYA

There are at least three different kinds of pieces for what is broadly labelled Theatre for Young Audiences, based on the ages of the target audience.

Although there can be different, more fluid groupings, or smaller, more specific target audiences, traditionally the three different age groups have been delineated as such: Little Kids (Kindergarten to Grade 3), Mid Kids (Grades 4 – 7), and Big Kids (Grades 8 – 12). Although I have also created shows specifically for young adults (aged 16 – 21), mostly this group is hard to access in a touring situation rather than just trying to attract them to "adult" venues.

The whole artistic creation for each group is somewhat different from each other, and one must find ways to present appropriate material in a way that is comprehensible for their age group, without ever being condescending or oversimplifying the content and how it's performed. Each group of kids — hell, every kid — is far more sophisticated and able to understand complexity more than many adults give them credit for. But the subject matter has to be relevant to their lives and what they are dealing with. However, any generalizations that one can attribute to any of these three groups as to how they respond might be refuted in different circumstances.

Content and Form

Most of the pieces I have directed in TYA have been based on an issue or issues of some sort, including bullying, racism, child poverty, restorative justice, ADHD, domestic violence, alcoholism, nuclear anxiety, and many more. But just because these plays deal with specific issues, it doesn't mean that they can't be exciting theatrically.

Like all "political" theatre, it is not the fact that it has a political imperative that makes it good or bad. Issue-oriented theatre for young audiences are the same. The issue/s that they confront can still be artfully told, using interesting theatricality, and employing all kinds of non-naturalistic styles to communicate its message.

As I mentioned earlier, political theatre — ALL theatre — works best when it tells a specific story about specific individuals. The audience will empathize with these characters' dilemmas if the focus is on them trying to deal with their specific circumstances, rather than creating a pamphlet on the issue. The issue is the backdrop to the action, even if — or perhaps especially if — it is the *raison d'être* for the show. The story is in the foreground. This is even more true when playing for young audiences.

Design

As I said earlier, I mostly prefer touring to schools or other centres rather than having a young audience in a theatre. Some of my most imaginative directing has been in school touring productions with miniscule budgets.

Yes, there is a "control" that you have in a theatre: house lights dimming to help create focus on the stage, no school bells or PA announcements sounding at inappropriate moments, no sweet sound of a crash bar when a student or teacher leaves the gym, no fighting against impossible acoustics, etc. But what you gain from transforming *their* space into a different world is irreplaceable.

When touring, you generally won't have lights, and if you do, they will be minimal and not terribly effective. Recently, I have been using video projections rather effectively, but generally, you want to rely on your best production element, namely imagination. There is often little time for set-up — usually no more than thirty minutes and usually done by the actors — and you certainly don't want to overburden them before they must perform in a space that generally needs greater physical and vocal energy than traditional venues.

You need to be extremely creative with design in a school touring show. Often the set needs to fit into a passenger van or small truck, so it can't be too large or it may not fit in the vehicle, and it must come apart and be reassembled quickly. There is often little time for costume changes during the show, and the costumes need to survive the wear and tear of two shows a day, five days a week, often in a high-energy show with its accompanying sweat. This is hit-and-run theatre, often with a running time of about forty-five to fifty minutes in order to fill a specific school time slot. You simply don't have the time, money or personnel for complicated designs to enrich your story.

In many ways, the "performance" starts the moment you enter the school, and does not finish until the moment you leave. How you interact with staff, teachers, and students is all part of the experience. Very often, you will have student helpers to help unload the set and costumes, help repack it after the performance, and perhaps help in other ways. How you deal with these students might literally inspire or change them for the rest of their lives.

Question and Answer Sessions

Too often, very little time, effort or focus is spent on this aspect of the presentation. They can be chaotic, unfocused, and ineffective. If they loved the show, the students might feel that this part is too much like being in class, and just want to get out of there now that the show is over.

I worked with Roseneath Theatre in Toronto for many years when it was run by David S. Craig. He is one of the premier TYA figures in Canadian theatre history. He has spent the vast majority of his career working in this sphere, and has spent countless hours thinking about this form.

Traditionally, it can sometimes be frustrating for the artists that the questions the kids might have are not about the content of the play, but about personal information about the actors, such as their age, if they've ever been on TV, what they do for a living (!), etc.

To counteract this, David developed a structure, based on a model created by Jerry Silverberg when he ran Cascade Theatre, that we would rehearse before we opened. There are three main parts to this structure:

1. We start with an introduction, led by one of the actors who has been designated as the leader — which might rotate every performance — and which would include any "housekeeping" information, such as production credits, funding acknowledgments, and the like. We conclude with each cast member introducing themselves and which part/s they played, finishing with the stage manager with an explanation of what they do. We also include a statement, if appropriate, such as, "We are all members of Canadian Actors' Equity Association, which means we are professionals who get paid for doing this, and this is our profession."

2. The leader would then say that they know the audience might have questions: about the script, the acting, the set, or anything else that interests them, but first, "we would like to ask YOU some questions." These are shared among the cast, sometimes dealing with their individual situation, such as, "In the play, my character, Sally, was confronted with a problem. Can anyone describe this problem in their own words?" They then ask for a show of hands, choosing someone by describing what they're wearing (do NOT say, "the boy in the Raptors T-shirt," because they might not be a boy!), and then repeat the answer that is given by the students so that everyone can hear.

   There are no right or wrong answers. All are valid. After the third answer to the question, say, "Thank you. Hands down." And move on to the next question. What one is trying to do is to start the discussion about the content of the play. About three or four of these questions should be enough. Obviously, these questions should be carefully constructed as to open up the issues without being judgmental, and thus encourage thoughtful answers from the students and perhaps stimulate starting points for further discussion later.

3. Finally, we get to the students' questions. Again, the answers should be shared amongst the cast. It is important to repeat the question, because often the students are nervous or embarrassed and will speak softly. If they then ask "personal questions," such as age, marital status, or how much you are being paid, you are totally within your rights to decline to answer, saying that that is a personal issue, and you don't feel comfortable answering it. If you don't mind answering, go ahead and do so.

If they ask how a bit of stage magic works, show them. There is nothing more magical than showing what is "up your sleeve." Often the questions might be about the process, such as, "How long did it take for you to make this piece?" Answer honestly, always including the writer, director, designers, production personnel, and administration staff who also worked on it.

It can be effective to get the student to answer their own question. For instance, if they ask, "Why did you decide to do this play?" you can ask them what they thought was the reason, or why they might think it's important to do a play about this subject matter.

If by any chance a child discloses some sensitive personal information, either in public or afterwards as you're getting ready to leave, listen thoughtfully and empathetically, but do not offer advice. You are not a social worker or psychologist. You are an actor. Ask for their name, and make sure you inform a faculty member, staff or principal about this person before you leave. Sometimes when dealing with sensitive issues, certain reactions might be triggered. The school needs to be informed that there might be a student who needs help.

Study guides, provided by the producing company, can be extraordinarily useful for teachers, helping them either before or after the show, giving ideas for activities, subjects for discussion, or even ways about how the students might create their own piece of theatre based on the themes of the play. But often the study guide is not even read by overworked, underpaid teachers, who see the play as a welcome respite from their classroom, or a chance to catch up on their marking. No matter how well written and conceived, one cannot rely on whether the study guide will ever be used.

Therefore, at the end of the Q and A session, encourage the students and teachers to talk about the play in class, and offer the students the option of writing the actors, director or playwright at the theatre's email with any comments or questions. Just make sure to answer them if they do.

Why TYA Is Vitally Important

The purpose of this work is NOT to build a future audience for the theatre. By producing high quality, relevant, exciting, and imaginative theatre for young people, and by engaging them with stories they can relate to, we are providing an opportunity for them to begin meaningful discussions — be it within the classroom, at the family dinner table, or with their peers — and contribute to thought-provoking examinations of the complexity of our modern world, which could help them navigate their own feelings and opinions about what they have just witnessed.

Every single person in our community deserves this resource. Unfortunately, not everyone has access to, or knowledge of, or even interest in what good, relevant, stimulating and provocative theatre has to offer.

It is a cliché to say that the hope for humanity lies in its youth. The best TYA can help shape new generations in a positive manner: encouraging them to question authority, to advocate for change, to empathize with those who might need help or understanding, and to empower them to reshape the world and their place in it.

14

New Plays

The process of breaking down the script into beats, asking questions, discussing backstory, investigating possibilities, engaging in a spirited debate about the world of the play and its themes, and choosing operative words is extraordinarily helpful in developing new scripts. Playwrights usually find it singularly revealing.

I think it is safe to say that most writers just...write. They try not to have too much of an agenda for the story or its characters pre-decided. Even if they have relatively detailed outlines, storyboards, scenarios, or "beat sheets," they still want to leave room for the spontaneous discovery that happens when the story takes off in unexpected directions. How many times have you heard a playwright say that their *characters* determined much of what occurred in a given situation, and not they, the writer?

Like many creative endeavours, the process is, by definition, highly instinctive. Who knows from where inspiration emanates, and when (or if) it will next appear? Most writers have experienced that rush of creativity when a certain passage or scene almost writes itself, and remains mostly intact, draft after draft, pretty well perfect from the moment it was committed to paper or screen. Now, these moments are often few and far between, which arguably makes them that much more special. The rest of the time, we slog away, wrestling with the ideas, dialogue and action that interests us, at least initially, painfully writing, then rewriting and rewriting and rewriting, relying on what techniques and experience we have gleaned along the way, trying to mould the work into acceptability, fighting off writer's block, attempting to encourage our best imaginations, until finally we must abandon the work to its deadline.

So, when someone who is the potential interpreter of this work starts from scratch, examining every beat, every word, every piece of punctuation — every strand — there is much that can be illuminating for the writer. What is clear? What is too clear? What are the clues to deciphering the intentions? Are there enough? Too many? Is it too easy for the actor to veer off in a wrong direction from what was intended? Is that a good thing or a bad thing? Etc., etc.

Now, in Canada, there are several ways new work is approached through workshopping. A half- or one-day workshop, a several-days to one-week workshop, a workshop production, or just a first production. Playwrights might actually experience all of the above during the development life of a new play.

The Dramaturg

Who is this person?

Back to our friend, the etymological dictionary: the word "dramaturg" is made from the word *drama* from the Greek "deed" or "to do," and *ourgos,* from the Greek for "work." A worker for the drama or, perhaps, for the dramatist.

Often, either due to economic necessity or preference, the director assumes this role when directing a new work. It is rare that a dramaturg is on staff or is hired on a freelance basis for a given project. When directing a new work, I prefer to be involved in the creation of the script as a facilitator/story editor/advocate for both the playwright and for what they are trying to say.

Reciprocally, I am happy for the writer to have some input in the first production, especially in casting. There is nothing quite so insecure as being a playwright during the production of one's work. The feeling of powerlessness is acute, as all these people are interpreting your creation that you have worked on so hard and for so long, while you watch helplessly on the sidelines. As the director, you can help ease this insecurity by involving the playwright whenever possible and listening to their concerns about any aspect of the production.

As a dramaturg, I will often meet with the playwright relatively regularly to check in on how the script is progressing before the production or workshop begins. The number of meetings will depend on how substantial the changes are and what the production or workshop deadlines might be. In the same way I have described being a mirror to the work of the actor, I try to do the same for the playwright. I similarly try to separate the work from the artist, responding to what I get from the material without judgment as to whether the writing is "good" or not. Again, be clear as to the intention versus what is actually on the page. Because the playwright is living constantly with their script, they often feel that certain things are obvious when they are not, or conversely, overwrite something that is patently clear and interestingly subtle.

My first question to a writer is always, "Why this play?" in the same way that I ask actors that question at the beginning of rehearsal. What was the inspiration to tell this story? What is the burning imperative that demands its creation? What kind of discussion or reaction would be your fantasy outcome from the audience witnessing it? And why a play, and not some other method of telling the story? In order to really get inside the material, the director/dramaturg and the actors must understand this initial impulse of the writer. All methods of realizing that impulse and the decisions on how to interpret it need to be based in many ways on that initial inspiration. It's a luxury to have a living playwright to access the text. Use it.

The main job of the director/dramaturg in a workshop situation is that of a facilitator, or a referee, or chairperson. Discussions can get bogged down, actors can become too prescriptive, playwrights too defensive, and the aims of the workshop can get lost. Issues with the text are repeated, and the same note is given by many and often. My standard is "Flag it, don't flog it." Once the playwright understands the note, move on.

The director/dramaturg must keep the activity on task, protect the playwright when necessary, separate the helpful from the unhelpful feedback, and/or steer the discussion away from other people trying to write the playwright's play. As for my personal input, unless I can insert it into the workshop, I will give those notes to the playwright away from a public forum in private. But if in the workshop, I make it a point to always try to frame the recommendation as a question (e.g., "Is it possible that this character is totally unaware of what is happening to them?")

That said, it must be made crystal clear to the playwright and everyone else that the writer always has the ultimate say. It is their work, and no one else's.

To Workshop or Not to…?

Why do some writers hate workshops? Based on my experience as an actor working on some of them, I can understand the sentiment. Again, there seem to be two kinds of bad workshop directors: those that encourage free-for-alls (Non-Directors), and those that eschew any actor input whatsoever (Over-Directors). Both are equally frustrating and more often than not, unhelpful to the development of the script.

In a free-for-all, the actors become script editors, or worse, playwrights; both positions which are counter to the very nature of acting. Even if the actor is a writer or dramaturg themselves (or perhaps especially if they are), the feedback that is most helpful to the writer is from an actor's point of view. The actor's perspective is, by definition, far more subjective and focused on their character, and not on the whole. It is far more valuable to the writer for an actor to say, "I'm confused as to why I suddenly lash out here," than to say, "Lashing out is a poor dramaturgical choice." The input needed from actors is "actor-ish."

With the latter type of workshop, the playwright misses out on a golden opportunity for actor input. After all, it is the actor who has to decipher, explore, interpret and ultimately perform these words. To find out what is clear and what isn't, what feels "playable" and what doesn't, and how the story of each character feels to the actor, can be wonderfully useful. In a sense, the actor becomes the advocate for their character, in the same way that the dramaturg should be the advocate for the playwright.

Of course, after a workshop process is an extremely valuable time to evaluate the script's development. It's also important to try to separate for the playwright what may have been lack of rehearsal time for the workshop actors to build their characters and decipher its intention from what needs to be clearer or deeper in the text. Writers may blame the actor for "not getting it," but it might be that the material was not gettable. Yet.

Now, I don't believe that everything has to be easy for the actor. Not everything has to be "clear." Some things are deliciously nebulous and complex. But there is an instinct that good actors have when those mysteries are exciting to explore, and when they are simply confusing. It falls to the dramaturg to help identify which is which and facilitate a useful discussion. Some actors are better at articulating their instincts than others. It doesn't make them better actors, just potentially more useful for workshops. I find it important to cast actors for workshops who are smart, articulate AND recognize the inherent difficulties and vulnerabilities of writing for the stage. They have to be sensitive to the fact that their words can be either devastating or uplifting to the writer.

In a production, the artistic impetus emanates from the playwright and moves towards the audience:

Writer → Director/Dramaturg → Designers → Actors → Audience

In a workshop, the direction of focus is reversed, usually minus the audience and designers:

Actors → Director/Dramaturg → Writer

In a production, most theatre artists would agree that our aim is to communicate with our audience; to move, entertain, provoke and otherwise engage them as completely as possible. In a workshop, we use our skills as theatre artists to aid, illuminate and otherwise engage the playwright, and to help them re-examine their work. But notice, the director is neither at the end nor at the beginning of the line in either formula. We are in the middle, more of a channel than initiator. The more accurate word might be facilitator.

The text is a blueprint. It does not truly exist until it is "built" — performed and witnessed by an audience. A workshop is the opportunity to keep on working on the blueprint before committing the time and resources to construct the production. The collaborative nature of the art form can reflect a collaborative process in its creation.

But some writers don't want that. At all.

Directing Your Own Play?

I say, in the vast majority of cases, no.

I also believe that it is totally inadvisable to direct a show in which you are acting, because you are trying to marry two distinct and unique functions: the subjective and the objective. These two functions are incompatible. It is ridiculously difficult to be objective about your own acting, and I would argue undesirable. Besides, there is a conflict of interest in directing your scene partner/s which will very possibly cause resentment. Your castmates will wonder if you are asking them to play something in order to put more focus on yourself or your character. The one exception to this situation might be if you have a co-director who may also be in the show and therefore you can direct each other. I have done that twice in my career.

Similarly, directing your own play contains two distinct functions — the creative and the interpretive — that cannot co-exist in one person simultaneously. In a production of a new play, it can be extremely challenging to determine if a problem with a passage is a writing issue or an acting/directorial one. Therefore, sometimes writer/directors will hire a separate dramaturg to help them, but personally, I would miss the collaboration of a director whose work I trust to interpret my work and perhaps inspire me to rewrite during the process, or to find a refreshing and unusual way to communicate what I have written.

You might consider directing your own work in a second or subsequent production of the play, after you, the writer, are relatively certain that all major rewrites are finished. And the playwright may feel that they can finally combat the helplessness they felt during the first production.

The Half-Day or One-Day Workshop

What can one do in such a short amount of time? Quite a bit, if managed correctly. Just make sure your goals are clear and achievable.

Obviously, you're going to read the script, probably only once. But how? With stage directions? If so, who reads them? The actors? You? Are you looking for flow? Then stage directions may be an impediment, unless they are actions that are essential to the story.

Before I start, I ask the playwright to give a short history about how they came to write the piece, and why they were inspired to write it as a play. I ask the cast if they have any questions that will affect the reading, usually having to do with meaning or intention, or if there is some information that they need to know in order to read it. You don't want to get into a lot of detail here, just what is needed for the read.

During the read, I will not hesitate to correct certain mistakes made by the actors if it affects meaning or intention. It's generally better to let it go, however, if it's minor and doesn't affect the sense, to get a sense of the length and the kind of pacing necessary for engaging storytelling.

After the reading, I will often get the actors to write down certain reactions which might be helpful to the writer. I get them to write them down so that the writer can take them away and study these comments or questions at their leisure, without any need to answer them in the workshop itself.

Examples are:

Three questions you have about your character.

Three things you like about the play.

Three questions you have about the story.

Three images from the play you find provocative.

Three words from your text that you see as a starting point to build your work.

What is the play about (in twenty-five words or less)?

One suggestion you might have for the writer (ONLY ONE!!!) about your character.

174 Text and Context

One thing you'd like your character to do or say.

Whose story is it?

Why is this an important story to tell?

Why did the playwright choose that particular title for the play?

Depending on the piece, you might ask fewer questions, more questions, or different questions.

If there's time, it might be useful to get the actors to read their answers out loud, as a possible starting point for discussion. It is imperative that this conversation NOT degenerate into suggestions for the writer on how they can rewrite their play. These are talking points only.

Equally important is to communicate to the writer that they do not need to answer or respond to this feedback. It may or may not be useful to them, and then only after they have had some time to digest it, in private, without any time pressure. This input is purely informational. It may be totally off base. That, in and of itself, may be useful for them to discover.

Lastly, I would get the writer to ask any questions they might have of the actors. This could be about anything, large or small, about how or if their intentions are being realized through the text.

The Three-to-Six-Day Workshop

As always, the first question is, "What does the playwright want to achieve?" With this length of workshop especially, but really with any workshop, I always expect that the script will move to its next stage of development as a result of our work. Clearly, any company that is willing to invest the significant amount of time and money required for a longer workshop will be anxious for some movement in its growth, although what that growth may be is hard to quantify.

With a three-to-six-day workshop, I feel I can do a slightly truncated version of the full operative word process I would in a full production situation. Through the parsing of the story and unravelling of its structure, playwrights learn a great deal about the narrative without anything being said. They may rewrite on their own based on this process. Similarly, the actors' choice of words and their character's journey can be incredibly informative to the writer.

Watching a playwright listen to their play using only the operative words is a wonderful experience. Again, this quintessential version of the text is not coming from out of the blue, but from the playwright's own words. Seeing their story play out, observing the conflicts between their characters, and listening to the actor advocate for the character they're portraying can be a powerful experience, and can inspire them to develop and/or deepen the work.

I might use questions to the playwright (as described in the one-day workshop process). Again, none of these reactions need be acted upon or even closely examined by the writer if they feel that the comments are irrelevant. I always hope that the writer will not rewrite too quickly. This is all just feedback, to be used or discarded as desired after due consideration.

It's important to keep hold of the principle that the workshop is process-oriented. Results may not be visible until much later, after the workshop is long over. That's fine. Yet again, there are no hard and fast rules for either plays or playwrights. Each workshop is unique; a writer may approach one of their plays differently than they'd approach another. Some playwrights embrace feedback, others don't. Even those whose initial reaction tends towards the defensive, may, given time and distance, come to see the value in the feedback.

Sometimes the playwright might want to see a particular section staged, or you as the director may want to stage a scene to see how it plays. This can be extremely useful, whether or not the staging is effective. Exposing difficulties or revealing confusions can be even more valuable than "successful" staging outcomes. We're looking for information, not results. Don't try to cover up difficulties or missing pieces. Exposing and confronting them will be much more helpful in the long run.

Perhaps improvising scenarios might be useful. Some of the improvisations I mentioned in Chapter 7 could be useful to the playwright, such as scenes we don't see but know about, "hot seat interrogations," or other made-up but relevant scenes. Again, solicit the playwright's input. There is no point in doing improvisations if the writer feels it is a waste of time.

I reiterate: you, as the director/dramaturg, are there to serve the writer. You might have disagreements with them, but it is their piece, and so ultimately, their final say. If you can't live with their decisions, or you feel strongly that the direction the script is taking is antithetical to your views or aesthetic, simply withdraw from the project after this developmental phase. Bullying the playwright to incorporate your viewpoint will help neither the script nor the writer nor you. You'll lose way more than you could possibly gain from this "victory."

Public Readings

Things change significantly when there is a public component as part of the process. The danger is that too much time and energy is spent on preparing for that, when the focus should only be on the script's needs. If there is a public reading, I try to limit any staging or "rehearsing." A simple setup of music stands, where perhaps the actor stands when they "enter" the action and sit when they "exit," and with somebody reading the necessary stage directions, is more than enough.

The worst that can happen is that the presentation falls between the stools of a staged piece and a reading. Actors on book scrambling with even minimal staging is excruciatingly boring. An audience loses the sense of the story by watching what would normally be a relatively chaotic phase of rehearsals, where the actor is trying to figure out movement, intention, contact with their fellow scene partners, physicality, etc. all at the same time. By limiting movement, the actor concentrates on the dialogue; their journey, the story, and their understanding of both their text and subtext. They shouldn't run before they know how to crawl.

I usually tend to read the stage directions myself, instead of inflicting some kind of performance anxiety on a stage manager or other non-performer. The stage directions are part of the rhythm of the reading and need intention and purpose, but not take focus. Choosing which stage directions to read should be considered carefully. For sure, less is more in this area. What you're looking for are only the ones that will help the listener understand the action they cannot see in a reading but will ultimately be able to when the play is staged.

Ironically, I can't tell you how often I've attended readings that were way more engaging theatrically than the fully staged and realized production. Perhaps it is the quintessential nature of the theatre for an audience to use their imaginations. There's less to be distracted by, and more concentration on the words themselves. The story can be more iconic, less "literal" than a full production. The experience is all about potential, and not limited by time constraints, money, or other factors that may disappoint rather than enhance.

This success, however, can be deceiving, unless one wants to keep the reading format as the end result. The production, fully staged and realized, which is way more difficult to achieve, is the breath that truly brings the work to life.

The Production Workshop

I have had about ten or so opportunities to do production workshops. I love them.

They were all between three and five weeks long, and usually included two to five presentations, with very discounted or pay-what-you-can admission prices. Sometimes, these "performances" were flexibly scheduled. In one process, which was five weeks long, we performed once after Week 3, twice after Week 4, and twice again at the end of Week 5. It's always beneficial to have time between presentations to make changes.

With structures such as these, true development, including audience reaction, can be allowed to occur without the pressure of a full production, with its accompanying reviews, opening night galas, Board of Directors receptions, and prayers to achieve, or even surpass, box office projections. The concentration in such a workshop can be on trying new things in front of people, including technical and design ideas as well as rewrites. Production workshops can even give artists the chance to change their minds, which is a luxury almost unknown in our producing system.

I approach this process in exactly the same way, using the text methodology and exercises described in Chapters 2 through 4. The removal of result-oriented goals allows all the participants to breathe easier. If I spend two weeks on the text work, it's not the end of the world. If we don't stage the last third of the play, it's not the end of the world. If the actors have to stay on book for a scene or section or even the whole piece, it's not the end of the world. If there are rewrites on the day of a presentation, that's fine. It's a proposal of how far we have been able to get to, and the audience LOVES being part of that process. They are what they should always be, a participant in the growth and maturation of the art and its content.

The First Production

One of the biggest questions when a new play is finally produced
is, "How long should the playwright keep rewriting?"

At a certain point, writers must abandon their work, as all
artists must. Most artists would never call their work "finished,"
especially not in such a process-driven art form as theatre. But
eventually we have to cease the creation phase and leave the piece
to the interpreters to fully inhabit, at least until there might be
an opportunity to tackle the work again, such as a remount or a
second production at another theatre.

It goes without saying that every playwright is different from
every other playwright. Some will rewrite forever, futzing and
worrying tiny details, or wanting to tackle huge issues, and
would happily do so until closing. Others come into rehearsals
with what they consider a production-ready draft and have no
interest in making any changes of any kind for this incarnation.
Of course, most playwrights are somewhere in between these
extremes.

The playwright and dramaturg must never forget that the actors
need stability and some sense of security. As much as we want to
keep the edges, we don't want actors to be only thinking about
rewrites or other changes in the show that will deter them from
"being there." I would never presume to say that all rewrites should
stop by opening night. But I would caution that any changes should
be able to be incorporated without causing any undue anxiety.
Anyway, some changes may just be what I call "sideways changes,"
in that they do not move the script forward, just sideways; not
better, just different.

After all, this is just the first production in what will hopefully
become many.

A Word of Caution

There is no one right way to write a play. There is no one right way to tell a story, or to reveal character, or narrative, or conflict, or anything else that a given play might contain. To say, "This is how plays are written" is limiting and presumptuous in the extreme.

I don't subscribe to certain vocabularies of dramaturgy that give names to certain aspects of narrative models, such as "rising action," or "overarching objectives," or any other nomenclature in this vein. I find terms such as these formulaic, and often will produce a structure that is equally formulaic and generic. Art isn't a "paint by numbers" process. It is messy, instinctive, and must be grappled with constantly to finally emerge into the light of day. Like casting, there is no scientific method or magic formula to either writing or facilitating the creation of a piece of theatre.

In the same way it is up to the director to find the most effective words for each individual actor, so too must you find the right language for each writer. If they don't seem to be understanding you, ask them if there is another approach that might be better for them. The relationship is arguably the most intimate of all one's collaborators in the theatre. You are in at the beginning of a new creation. You are their advocate, their champion.

The dramaturg can provide invaluable feedback, as long as it's not in the context of "this is what plays are," or "this is how stories are told." The best image is that of a midwife, helping the writer birth their work, facilitating the writer's imagined world, and providing valuable feedback as to whether the writer's intentions are being realized.

But like all good facilitators, the first task is to identify what the writer wants to say, and why they are interested in saying it, and then help them do just that.

15

Devised Work

I have facilitated/dramaturged/directed about a dozen devised pieces in my career, and I always feel like they extract a small part of my soul in their creation, never to be recovered. It is also a very different type of directing, and unique in its demands.

Groups that have devised their own work for years, or artists that work in this way with other artists, have created a process that works for them. It would be rare that they would bring in an outside director/facilitator who was not part of their ongoing process. And so almost all of the devised work I have led has been with theatre school students or young professionals.

I believe there are three stages for the leader of this process:

1) Facilitator — helping the participants get at and express their theatrical ideas,

2) Dramaturg — helping the participants shape and hone their work, and

3) Director — helping the participants stage and present the work.

These are a few of the precepts in my process:

1) Decisions must be made by consensus. No voting will occur.

2) Everyone must contribute. Everybody must speak.

3) Every individual is responsible for their own agenda in the work, and as such needs to be heard.

4) Often, the most contentious issue in the creation process reveals the real conflict of the content of the piece.

5) Collective groups are better at creating theatrical pieces than they are at writing "plays." Don't look for a well-made play from a group. But it can still be an exciting piece of theatre.

Democracy

Most frustratingly, this work is — at least as I define it — an exercise in democratic collectivism. There is only one irrefutable quality of democracy: it is hell. True democracy — not what passes for the governance of our country's government, but real participatory democracy, where decisions must be made with the full approval of ALL — is time-consuming, contentious, and can produce some very raw emotions and seemingly irreconcilable conflicts.

If it is truly a "collective creation" (this was the name of the genre used in the '60s and '70s in Canada when it was developed by visionaries such as Paul Thompson at Theatre Passe Muraille), then the collective must all create equally, with an honest yet respectful communication. Some people are natural loudmouths and take up a lot of space. (Guilty, Your Honour.) Others are quiet, more reserved, and better listeners. Some possess both these qualities at different times. Some are supremely self-confident about what they have to say. Others, not so much.

It is absolutely vital that the facilitator keep track of all of the participants and insist that everybody have their say. It is not good enough for a less confident person to say, "I agree with so-and-so." They must express why they agree with them and exactly with what they are agreeing. Everyone must contribute actively, not just passively.

This can be difficult, to say the least. True listening is not easy, and most of us have been trained to communicate our ideas and defend them rather than to really listen. We sometimes mistake true listening for waiting for the other person to stop talking so that *we* can begin to start talking.

The process of how the group creates and presents the material needs regular assessment and reassessment. Problems or resentments within the group need to be confronted. Conflicts within the group, if handled with honesty and respect, can be healthy, not to mention illuminating (see #4 in the precepts list above).

Now, I also believe that devised work needs a leader...in other words, a director. It is hard, although not impossible, for a collective group to direct themselves. They have enough to do in creating, shaping, collaborating and performing their piece without the objective task of directing.

But, make no mistake, one is directing a new work created by this entity of collective artists, and as in all new works, the writer(s) may have some input into the general "direction" that the piece follows. The leader is the facilitator. The collective is the writer and performer. Another difficult balancing act.

Getting Started

As always, starting with questions is a good idea: Why is this piece devised? What does that mean, anyway? Are all the participants up for the challenge? What's the starting point, if any? Does everybody agree to participate fully and adhere to the basic rules? Are they up for participating in a true democratic process?

All of these questions and more must be addressed before the work even begins. Devised work demands more from everyone involved. Actors are also creators. Designers must have the patience of Job, because they cannot design a jot until there is a script, or at least a story, or at least a theatrical idea. Stage managers become recorders and transcribers, as well as trying to keep track of all the ephemeral ideas and brainstorming sessions. And nobody knows anything for a very long time into the process, often not until mere days before the first performance.

If you're starting with a theme, or subject matter, or image, or any other starting point, you're ahead of the game. Homework, writing assignments, interviewing potential experts or relevant witnesses are all possible. But if you're told, "Create a piece with this group, please," as has happened to me several times, then the first order of business is to find out what this group wants to talk about.

First Steps

Months or even weeks before rehearsals begin, I will try to meet with the group. I want to get to know these individuals as quickly as possible. If they know each other well, like a class of theatre students, I will get them to introduce each other. In a circle, one of the participants introduces the person to the left of them, and tells me any relevant information, such as where they come from, their background, their likes and dislikes, their hobbies, their personality, etc. The person being described can add to or correct any information provided. We then move to the next person in the circle, who introduces the person to their left. If the group doesn't know each other, divide people into groups of two, get them to talk to each other for fifteen minutes or so and exchange information about each other, and then they will introduce each other to the whole group. This is a good exercise for sharing, listening, and retaining information. Of course, I also introduce myself.

Then I often give the participants writing exercises. It's important not to put too much pressure on these and encourage the creators/ cast to not write volumes. Often, a couple of paragraphs, or fifty words or less can be good guidelines. The point, partially, is to debunk some of the mythology surrounding writing. Everyone can write. And everyone needs to be encouraged to write. What the writing exercises are about may or may not be related to the starting point, if any. It can be a "fill in the blank" structure, such as, "When I was 12, my secret desire was to be _____." Or, "I am most frustrated when _____." Lists can be useful, such as, "Name twenty-five roles you play (e.g., parent, child, sibling, co-worker, etc.)." Or, "Name twenty-five words to describe you (e.g., left wing, volatile, judgmental, myopic, etc.)" Direct statements can be useful, such as, "If this piece says one thing, I'd want it to be _____."

If you're not starting with anything, these exercises can be a useful way of getting the individuals in the group writing about what is important to them. The questions might be about priorities in life and/or art, politics, love, ethnicity, sexual identity, etc. It's important to communicate that the participants must be willing to share the work, out loud, and possibly as part of the piece-to-be, but that any of this work may or may not be used in the creation of the piece. It might just be useful as a way to start the writing engine.

As any writer will tell you, the hardest part of writing...is writing. It's important just to get at stuff, without judgment or wondering how it fits in to any kind of story or thematic imperative. Encourage them to put the objective, judging part of the brain on hold. Getting individuals into the habit of writing constantly in this process is helpful. They may not be used to using this muscle, or if they are, not in this way. This is hit-and-run writing: quick, emotive, and dirty (in that it is not refined and honed). The point is to see if there is an idea or image or even a phrase that is worth developing later.

As most writers will attest, a deadline is your best friend. Assignments with deadlines help create arguably the most important aspect of this kind of work. For example, on a specific date, there will be an audience coming to see this piece, and we better have something to show them. Or, these writing exercises are due in three days.

Starting the Day

Of course, every process of devising, like every devised project, is different. The process must change as the factors involved in each project dictate. That said, what follows is a process I have used quite a few times over the last twenty years or so.

I start every day with exercises to establish and deepen collectivism, as well as individual exploration. Some of these are:

1) **The Name Game**: The group stands in a circle and establishes a rhythm. One person says another's name and takes their place in the circle. That person says another's name and takes that person's place, etc. The aim is to never let the rhythm drop, and the whole group, and each individual in it, is responsible for that. You can call the person's name who called yours, if need be. As the group gets good at that, add their last names. Later, their middle names. Perhaps a nickname. Now everybody knows everyone else's full, "real" name, complete with however many middle names anybody might have.

2) **Clapping**: A continuous stream of clapping the numbers 1–9. There are two sets of each number, except for "9," which is repeated 4 times before returning back to "8" and downward to "1."

The key is accents, as there is no break between numbers. The accent is on:

> The first beat on the sets of "1," "2" and "3,"
> The first and third beat of "4,"
> "5" is a group of three followed by a group of two,
> "6" is two groups of three

"7" is one group of three, followed by two groups of two, "8" is two groups of three, followed by one group of two, and "9" is three groups of three.

It's complicated and takes immense concentration. When it first starts, most people drop out after a short while, losing their place as to where they are in the pattern. After a few weeks, most everyone begins to get it, and when the whole group manages to get it and finish exactly on the beat together, the feeling is euphoric. Great for collaborating skills.

3) **Frogs**: The phrase "One frog, two eyes, four legs, kerplunk, in the puddle" is the basis of this game. A rhythm is established by lightly slapping one's thighs for two beats, lightly clapping for two beats, and snapping fingers for two beats.

One person in a circle says. "One frog." The next, "two eyes," and so on, going around the circle in sequence. After "in the puddle," the next person says, "two frogs," the next, "four eyes," the next, "eight legs," the next, "kerplunk," the next, another, "kerplunk," the next, "in the puddle," followed by the next saying, "in the puddle." We move to three frogs, with the corresponding number of eyes and legs, and as many "kerplunks" and "in the puddles" as there are frogs, each one being said by the next person in the group. Again, concentration, listening, breathing and being part of the group are the aims to this ridiculous but incredibly difficult game. Everyone is responsible, and success or lack of success belongs to the whole group. At the beginning, it is common not to get beyond two or three frogs. By the end of three weeks, it is possible to get to ten or more.

These might sound like early theatre school games. In a way, they are. But we are really starting from scratch to create something with a group that has presumably never created one piece collectively before. Trust, group rhythm, unified purpose, collective and individual responsibility, not to mention fun, must be built from the ground up. Unless this group has created devised work before, they need to start at zero.

I do other exercises as well, which might morph into improvisations. One, devised by Joanne Akalaitis, is called "Walking Through Your Life." The participants move around the space, without speaking or demonstrating anything, and spend 60 seconds in every year of their life. The facilitator says, "You are now 0 years old," 60 seconds later, "You are now 1 year old," 60 seconds after that, "you are now 2 years old," etc. You can only go as high as the youngest participant. This exercise can be particularly useful if the piece you are working on is trying to access a certain age.

It is important for the participants not to "act" being whatever age they are in the exercise. By spending a minute per age, we are looking to access certain specific physical memories, although it is unlikely that anybody remembers much of anything as an infant or toddler. That said, it is surprising what may occur unbidden to the participants.

I directed/facilitated one project for Humber College where the group was devising a Theatre for Young Audiences piece for Grades 4–7. We decided to set the age of the characters at twelve, so every morning we would "walk through" their lives until twelve, then stay at that age, moving into various scenarios (school, recess, etc.), or locations (home, the bus, etc.), or activities (watching TV, playing sports, etc.). At times, there might be interactions with others; at other times, not.

It's not easy to be authentic when playing an age younger than you are now. Like our examination of words, age, as expressed as a number, has a ton of baggage, and must be examined viscerally, not intellectually. The feelings of insecurity, awkwardness, unbridled energy, growing pains, oncoming puberty and others mostly manifest themselves physically, followed by the psychological. By literally walking through to become that age on a daily basis, the participants can begin to remember, on a very primal and specific level, exactly what that age was for them.

Next Steps — Improvising Scenes

It's time to start to create material.

There are myriad ways to get the group to start improvising scenes. One way is to do the Name Game again, but this time get everybody to rename themselves. It could be how you're feeling today ("Anxious," "Tired," "Excited," etc.). Play the game where these are now their names. See if the rhythm can be maintained with these names. Or they could name themselves by an issue or theme they want to deal with in the piece (racism, inequity, change, etc.).

Depending on the size of the whole group, you then want to divide up into smaller groups. Decide how large a group you want to start them working together — between three and five is usually a good starting point — and wherever everybody ends up at the end of the Name Game, they number themselves. For instance, if there are twenty-five in the whole group, they go in one direction and number off from 1 to 5. Then all the 1s work together, all the 2s, etc.

To begin with, the text is the words they chose for this last session of the Name Game, and ONLY those words. Like our operative word exercise, every word must be said at least once, but no more than three times. In this case, anybody can say any word, not necessarily their own, but no other words may be used. Sounds, such as machine noise, or animals, or other sound effects are exceptions.

There are instructions in the creation of these scenes:

1) There must be a clear beginning and end to the scene.

2) The point of view of the group must be evident in the scene created.

3) It must have a title.

4) They must work together, collaboratively and respectfully. They must listen to all ideas, and everybody must contribute.

Their starting point is their "text" of words and what scenario might suggest itself to the group. And they have fifteen minutes before presenting their scene to the rest of the group!

After viewing the scenes, the whole group gets to discuss briefly what they thought was successful, and what was perhaps unclear or confusing. There should also be a quick check-in about the process; whether it was efficient, inclusive and creative — or not. Then, very importantly, somebody or a group of participants needs to be designated as recorders. It is their job to briefly describe the scenes in writing, giving them a number and the title chosen, and listing who was in the scene.

There are other tasks that need looking after by the group: cleaning the space, communication, perhaps being a *liaison* with the design departments, or whatever seems appropriate. Every participant should have one of these additional "housekeeping" duties.

So, after the fifteen-minute rehearsal, perhaps fifteen minutes of presentation (hopefully no scene is longer than a minute or two), and another fifteen minutes of discussion, the group has five scenes in its library. In this way, scenes can be created quickly, looking for the essence of a story, or theme, or thesis, or something that will hopefully start to emerge.

There are many ways to get at source material for these improvised scenes: the writing exercises they did before rehearsals, renaming in the Name Game based on different themes, the newspaper, conversations overheard on the street, etc. Source material exists everywhere.

The key is to never let the participants "write" too much for these improvs. Limit the number of words. After graduating from just using one word each, maybe it's time for whole sentences in which at least one of the words must be included. I will sometimes limit them to only ive lines of dialogue. The short rehearsal for the scenes also helps. Encourage creative solutions, such as huge physicality, the interpretation of inanimate objects or concepts by actors, theatrical solutions to challenges of place, time, and cast size, etc.

It's also important to vary the size of the groups creating these scenes, although I tend to resist one-person scenes for the time being. Groups from two to the full complement and every permutation in between are good to explore. Dividing by gender identification, age, geography, or any other factor could be tried. What you're looking for is that everyone works with everyone, and their partners are completely chosen at random.

> I worked at the National Theatre School using this process, and several weeks in, I asked the entire group of twenty-seven first-year actors, directors, production students, playwrights and designers to create one scene all together for the first time in the process. I gave them the theme of the conflict between unity and disunity. I left them alone for about twenty minutes. When I returned, I was greeted with chaos. Several rushed up to me, in a panic, saying how awful this scene had gone. There were arguments all over the place. A few were seated separately, heads in their hands. Some were crying. There were arguments and blame. It was chaos. I of course was madly trying to figure out how I could repair the damage and rebuild trust and support for each other.
>
> Finally, after a minute or two of this, a lone person sat depressed in the middle of the floor. Slowly, gradually, they were joined by another person who put their hands on them for comfort, then another, then another, until the whole group created this beautiful tableau, everyone in physical contact, still and silent. It could not have been a more perfect realization of the assignment, and although this scene itself was not part of the finished piece, its creation did more for bringing the group together than

> any other moment. The fact that I was totally sucked into
> the ruse was a moment of triumph for the WHOLE group,
> and an invaluable asset in moving forward with their
> process of collective creation.

After, say, three weeks of this stage, it's probable that there might
be anywhere between seventy and one hundred scenes that have
been created, more than enough to start building a "play."

Structure

As we are building our stockpile of scenes, almost concurrent to
that is the gradual emergence of a possible narrative structure, or
at least, a framework for the scenes.

After a few days of creating scenes, I ask that everyone take some
time (a few days or so) and individually write an offer to the group
as to a possible structure on which to hang our work. There is
usually a huge array of offers. Some might want the traditional
narrative of a "well-made play." Others, a stream-of-consciousness
dream.

Each member of the group makes their offer of the structure to the
whole group. They should title their proposal, and have it written or
printed to submit to the library of material, under a new category
of "structure," and a letter assigned to differentiate them from the
numbered scenes. There might be a short discussion of the merits
of each offer after each presentation. There is no need to criticize
any of them at this point in the process. Keep it all positive.

The process now becomes reducing the number of offers.
Depending on the number of participants, I usually ask them to
ally themselves with one or two others in the group with whom
their offers seem to mesh. Again, presuming a group of twenty-
five, that might mean anywhere between eight and twelve new
groups. And the process is repeated.

Several days later, we have new proposals from these new groups, each with a title and letter, and followed by a discussion, still in the positive vein. And we repeat. Often by this point, we may be able to get it down to two, three or four groups.

> My favourite way of a group choosing partners is silently. At Humber, a participant suggested that people just arrange themselves into three groups, without talking or making any sound, with people they felt most allied to in terms of their proposals. Three corners of the room were chosen for these alliances to be created. What resulted was almost a dance, as different groups formed, disbanded, re-formed, traded places, lost or gained individuals, and otherwise silently negotiated themselves into three equal-sized groups. It only took about twenty minutes, but it was a fantastic way of choosing one's proposal partners.

By now, certain themes have almost certainly begun to emerge. Individuals will have been stating their priorities as to what they desire to see this piece deal with. I make sure to reiterate that each participant is responsible for their own agenda. If they want the piece to deal with a certain issue or theme, it is up to them — with the facilitator's help, of course — to ensure that it is included.

Very often, as we get down to fewer and fewer groups, content and form are beginning to merge. If a participant is allying with a certain group, it often has to do with what is being proposed as content, as opposed to how it's being said. But of course, there are always exceptions to prove this rule. Whatever structure is being proposed by a group, it will almost certainly have to encompass a range of themes or issues.

So finally, after two or three weeks, there are just a few proposals left, usually between two and four. They each, presumably, have their strengths and weaknesses. It can be helpful to get it down to two proposals, but not absolutely necessary. Often, I will simply ask the whole group to fold the remaining proposals into one.

Sometimes it becomes absolutely clear to the group that one proposal far outweighs the others, and everyone feels they can work within that structure — perhaps with some amendments — to achieve their priorities and be satisfied with the framework.

It's also possible to leave it at two proposals for now. Is there a way that the final framework can encompass both? Can the dynamic of two opposing frameworks actually be part of the piece? Is that the framework that everybody's agenda can be dealt with satisfactorily?

Culling

Around this time, say perhaps into the first part of Week 4, depending on your time constraints, we have amassed a significant amount of material and hopefully one or two possible structures. The next step is to sift through the material to see what is germane to the emerging themes and structure.

Time to talk through them all. Every scene has been recorded, and their description, title and participant list are now read out. Some of them were a while ago. What we thought was fantastic, in retrospect and with the passage of time, may not be all that interesting. Or the reverse. Something that people were not totally enthused about suddenly seems to be an important germ of an urgent idea in the emerging nature of our piece.

This is where discussions can get intense. Obviously, there can be wildly divergent points of view on different scenes. Sometimes, people love the intention, even if the execution was somewhat lacking.

It's time to divide all the scenes into three main groups:

1) **Keepers** — everybody really likes this scene and feels it is vital to be included, perhaps with some changes.

2) **Idea Keepers** — people liked something about this scene, but not perhaps in its present form. It might be its thematic intention, an idea it presented, an image that emerged, a line or word that resonated, etc. It should stay, but it needs lots of work.

3) **Discards** — nobody sees anything really worth keeping in these scenes.

In my experience, it usually breaks down to 25% for Keepers, 50% for Idea Keepers, and 25% for Discards. That would still leave way too much material, but it is after all only a first cull. Still, draconian measures are encouraged. It's time to be brutally honest about the merits, or lack of same, in each scene.

Sometimes there also might be a scene that has not been created, but its potential existence has been identified and prioritized. For instance, the actors of colour may want a scene that only includes them, but we have never had a chance to create one as yet. It gets added to the pile of Keepers, assuming there is consensus for its creation.

Again, no votes are taken. Every scene is talked through until consensus is reached. All it takes is one person to advocate for a scene, even if everyone else wants it discarded, and the discussion continues until that person has either convinced everybody else enough to hang on to it — at least as an idea — or until that person has been convinced to discard it. It may be that the scene in question, or what that person saw in it, can be folded into another scene. Or maybe this impasse is unresolvable for now. In that case, the scene becomes part of that person's agenda to ensure its continued existence in the piece.

There is no need to solve every problem, or resolve every contentious issue, especially if it is a theoretical one. If two factions have different ideas that seem incompatible, a way forward is always to try both options and see what happens. Certain unresolved discussions, such as "What do we want this piece to be about?" can stay unresolved. Remember, the conflict in the group may actually be useful to the content, and/or become part of the narrative.

Design

Concurrent to this is to begin to talk to your designers. Hopefully, there is enough of the possible content and form of the piece to start this process, at least in general terms. You might have a possible location that can act as a base to return to, or an idea of how to create many different locations as needed with minimal transitions, or a non-naturalistic image that could be anywhere. You might want all the actors wearing a kind of uniform costume, or at least variations on a thematic image. You may want to use existing music, or utilize the musicianship of the group to create a soundscape.

The point is to get started on the designs now that you know a bit more about where the piece is headed. Whatever the ideas are, they must be quickly executed, and still leave room for the inevitable changes that will come. It will be helpful for the designer/s to be in rehearsal as much as possible, to see what the process has been and what progress is being made. Then your discussions with them will have a context, even though there is still no script *per se*.

Draft 2

The next step is to try to develop the Keeper and Idea Keeper scenes to their next draft stage. Participants have to choose which scenes to work on, since now is the time to work on material concurrently. Depending on the number of people required for certain scenes, several scenes can be worked on at the same time. This can be a complicated logistical problem, as most actor/creators want to work on almost everything. But choices have to be made, so sometimes they must give up working on one thing in order to work on another. In other words, they must establish what is most important to them.

A schedule is made to get to all these scenes with the people who want to work on them as efficiently as humanly possible, in say two to three days. They need more time now to work on these scenes. They need to be deeper, smarter, and reveal why they are important. A half hour or so, perhaps? Not too much longer than that, as there is a ton of stuff to get through. When done, these new drafts are presented, perhaps with a new title and a number which designates it as a second draft (version 2.0?), discussed, and recorded.

Now the discussion must also include the added factor of how — or even if — it fits into the whole. It might be a great scene for another play. Or as the participants worked on it (remember, this was a priority for the individuals of this group), they lost interest in it. They now advocate that it be discarded. Or sometimes, it becomes clear that a given scene is very much like another one. Can they merge? Do we really need two scenes so similar to each other? Or are they different enough to warrant both of them staying?

Hopefully after this second-draft stage, things are becoming somewhat clearer. More scenes have been discarded or merged with others, we're down to one or two structures, and certain themes are emerging. But time is getting short. It might be ten days or so until the "opening."

It's now time for a most shocking strategy.

Leaving

I leave.

Usually for twenty-four hours. And as I leave, I say, "I am the director of this piece. But I don't have a piece to direct. I will give you twenty-four hours to structure, order and shape your piece. I will return this time tomorrow, and I would like to see a complete run-through of the piece at that time. And also, give it a title. Good luck!" And with that, I leave the hall, usually seeing a lot of open-mouthed, disbelieving, and sometimes angry participants.

Hopefully, processes have been established about collaborative working methods. Hopefully, leadership is shared. Hopefully, they are now used to deadlines, having had some serious time constraints for the last few weeks. Hopefully, they know how to make decisions, or at least try several different ways of moving forward.

I always leave with trepidation, afraid that things will fall apart, or that the participants will fail to meet the deadline. But neither fear has ever been realized. Somehow, they pull together, and when I return, I am always amazed and moved as to how much they've achieved in such a short amount of time.

Now, of course, what they've presented to you is far from perfect. It is simply a draft of the whole piece. Certain scenes may just be sketched in, others too detailed, or there may be holes in the framework, and the whole thing is almost certainly too long.

So, we have another critique session, and analyze just exactly what there is and how it can be improved, as well as how it was achieved. Over and above an examination of each bit and the overall structure, does everyone feel included? Is their agenda being dealt with? Are there scenes missing? Does the order feel appropriate? Is it clear? Too clear? Is there a build? Does it all potentially add up to something interesting? If not, why not? Difficult questions, and again, not all of them need answers right away.

Now is the time for the dramaturg to really kick in, followed closely by the director. So far, you've been mostly facilitating the creation. But thankfully, you are now outside it. You've just watched this new creation with fresh eyes, not having been present for this synthesis. Be honest but understand the context. Be positive, but rigorous.

Rehearsal

So now we can rehearse. Finally. Starting from the beginning, we begin a work-through, dealing with everything all at once:

dramaturgy of the scene, its place in the framework, the staging, character development, and the acting needed to communicate the scenes. It's a lot all at once, but there's not a lot of time.

There will be rewrites. Does a certain participant want to take on a certain scene by themselves, or with a select group of a few others? Are there monologues? Should the person speaking it write it? Do some scenes need to be improvised again? And what about those scenes that have been identified as priorities but have yet to be created? Does the order of the scenes make sense?

I always make sure to be very clear from the beginning that the collective is NOT directing the piece. Everyone has input, where and when appropriate, but there are just too many things to do and problems to solve to take the time it usually takes to make certain directorial decisions by consensus. Unless you have months of rehearsal, and not weeks, what is needed now is some benevolent dictatorship. You don't have to be an asshole, but some clear experienced leadership is desirable at this point. This is why you must be clear at the very beginning of the process about your role in this collective. You are the director. They are the creator/performers.

It is possible, but not easy, that you can get through this rehearsal stage in about a week, followed by a run-through, followed by some more discussion and changes. This hopefully leaves you a few days to rehearse again, tech the show and run it through once or twice more before an audience views it. Yes, it's exhausting. And as I said, it usually takes a chunk of your soul. It will probably be a race to the finish to get there in time. But as Geoffrey Rush's character says in *Shakespeare in Love*, "It all turns out well. [How?] We don't know. It's a mystery."

Why Go Through this Hell?

What results more often than not is a piece of theatre in which the participants feel ownership, both figuratively and literally. It reflects who they are — as a group, and as individuals — instead of trying to interpret someone else's world and artistic vision. It can deal with the burning issues of the day and confront what they themselves most feel the need to confront. And they wrote every word of it; together and individually. It will have an excitement and urgency that this ownership engenders.

This experience is irreplaceable for young artists. It can literally empower them to rethink the process of creating theatre. It might place them along a path of creating their own work. It might challenge preconceptions of thinking of the actor as clay that needs moulding, or a pawn in some other artist's grand vision. It gives them a voice and an opportunity to think of theatre as an immediate response to the world and their place in it, and that they can create this response with other young artists.

In short, they become creators, and not only interpreters.

Afterword

So, that's it. My book. I hope at least some of you found at least some of it somewhat helpful.

One of the good things about growing older is feeling less and less like you have to prove something, or that you need to demonstrate that you belong to the professional cadre of artists. It's mostly all about the work now, and not about my place in it. That will have to be judged by others — if at all — when I'm dead, and I won't give a shit about it then.

At this juncture, I want to experience as many different processes as possible. There are infinitely more stories to tell about difficult, complex subjects, and an urgent need to tell them. I trust my instincts and experience, but still strive to listen better and learn new things.

People have been forecasting the demise of theatre for well over a hundred years. First, it was the cinema that was going to make theatre obsolete, then radio, then television, and now the internet, livestreaming and on-demand programming. Soon it will be micro-chips in our brains...or something. And then there might be a global pandemic which will impede public gatherings.

But theatre won't die. It can't possibly, because it fills an immutable need in us all; an undeniable thirst that we humans have to gather together in groups to view and participate in live events, be it music or dance or political rallies or theatre, even if we do so at a social distance from each other. And in the impending apocalypse, theatre will really show its worth as the most economical and immediate method to respond to our world and to feed our need to collectively hear the stories that must be told.

I have never lost my love for this art form. It has sustained me for my entire career. I have never wanted to seriously delve into any other medium. To me, the art form is endlessly fascinating, because it is so quintessentially naive, and therefore limitless. It is based on imagination. It needs only our own creativity to fuel it. It demands a willingness from its audience to enter into a different world, even though we all know it's completely made-up, in order to learn more about the "real" world. It reconnects us to the awe and wonder of our childhoods.

What greater gift can an art form give?

Richard Greenblatt

Toronto 2021

Acknowledgments

Peter Hinton shared with me some of the writing exercises and games used in the devised text chapter. Perry Schneiderman and I exchanged many improvisations and exercises. Ben Bennison was my improvisation teacher at RADA, and a great inspiration to me.

Many actors I have worked with over the years have taken to the text methodology with great energy and enthusiasm, and from them I learned much. They helped to shape what is written in these pages. They are too numerous to name, but I am extraordinarily grateful to them all.

These friends and colleagues read drafts of this work and gave me invaluable feedback: Colin Rivers, Julie Tepperman, Kelly Wolf, Pam Winter, Celia Chassels, Dennis Foon, Judith Thompson, Dixie Seatle, David S. Craig, and Ali Joy Richardson.

I am indebted to J. Gordon Shillingford Publishing, with special thanks to my editor Glenda MacFarlane for her unwavering support and sage advice throughout the publication process.

My brother Lewis Furey, who has always been a fierce supporter of me and my work, had many valuable observations.

My theatrical sister Diane Flacks is always one of my best critics and an unconditional ally.

My daughter Natasha Greenblatt is a fantastic employer of the text method and was my greatest spur in writing this book. She also read the very first draft and gave me fantastic and useful feedback.

My son Will Greenblatt is an ever-vigilant referee of my wayward thoughts and fuzzy thinking. He was indispensable in providing editorial and grammatical help to this work.

My late son, Luke Greenblatt, was a deep soul, and taught me how to listen more and better.

My daughter Amelia Greenblatt, who loves language as fiercely as she lives life, is a constant challenge and inspiration.

My beloved wife Tanya Greve keeps me grounded and honest and is always my first and most trusted editor.

Special thanks to all those who read and offered their endorsement of this book: Keith Barker, Geoff Bullen, Andrea Donaldson, Jillian Keiley, Jani Lauzon, Seana McKenna, Alisa Palmer, Carey Perloff, Miles Potter, Guillermo Verdecchia, and Kelly Wolf. A very special thank you to Judith Thompson for her beautiful foreword and permission to use the excerpt from *Lion in the Streets*.

I was at RADA in the same class as Alan Rickman. We shared a flat for most of my time in London with several other people, including his partner, Rima Horton. We would talk long into the night, smoking and dreaming and formulating our ideas and arguing and, basically, becoming theatre artists. He was a great influence on my life and my art, as he told me I was to him. I miss him tremendously, and I think that he would be happy that this book exists.

Here's to a healthy and equitable future.

Richard Greenblatt

Richard Greenblatt was born and raised in Montréal and trained as an actor at The Royal Academy of Dramatic Art in London, England. He returned to Canada in the mid-70s and has been working as an actor, director, writer, musician, and educator ever since. His work has taken him across the country, throughout the U.S., and to Europe and Japan. The vast majority of his extensive directing work has been with the development and premières of original scripts, quite a few of which were for Theatre for Young Audiences. He has written and performed two solo shows *(Soft Pedalling* and *Letters from Lehrer),* co-authored two plays with Diane Flacks *(Sibs* and *Care),* and co-authored the immensely successful *2 Pianos 4 Hands* with Ted Dykstra, which they performed almost 1,000 times and has been seen around the world in hundreds of other productions. Greenblatt has directed and taught acting and directing at most of the top training institutions in Canada and is the recipient of numerous Dora and Chalmers Awards. He lives in Toronto.